Management Accounting Research in Practice

Lessons Learned from an
Interventionist Approach

Petri Suomala and Jouni Lyly-Yrjänäinen

Routledge
Taylor & Francis Group

NEW YORK   LONDON

First published 2012
by Routledge
711 Third Avenue, New York, NY 10017

Simultaneously published in the UK
by Routledge
2 Park Square, Milton Park, Abingdon, Oxon OX14 4RN

*Routledge is an imprint of the Taylor & Francis Group,
an informa business*

Typeset in Sabon by IBT Global.

Library of Congress Cataloging-in-Publication Data
Suomala, Petri, 1974–
    Management accounting research in practice : lessons learned from an
interventionist approach / By Petri Suomala and Jouni Lyly-Yrjänäinen.
    p. cm. — (Routledge studies in accounting ; 10)
    Includes bibliographical references and index.
    1. Managerial accounting.—Research. 2. Managerial accounting.
    I. Lyly-Yrjänäinen, Jouni, 1976–   II. Title.
    HF5657.4.S846 2011
    658.15'11072--dc23
    2011027811

ISBN: 978-0-415-80677-0 (hbk)
ISBN: 978-0-203-14120-5 (ebk)

Contents

PART I:
Ten Years of Interventionist Research

PART II:
Selected Research Projects

PART III:
Lessons Learned

Tables

Figures

Abbreviations

ABC	Activity-Based Costing
ATO	Assembly to Order
BOM	Bill of Materials
CAD	Computer-Aided Design
CMC	Cost Management Center
ETO	Engineer to Order
FDF	Finnish Defence Forces
IOCM	Inter-Organisational Cost Management
IV	Interventionist
LCC	Life Cycle Costing
MA	Management Accounting
MTS	Make to Stock
OBA	Open Book Accounting
OEM	Original Equipment Manufacturer
PAFF	Prevention, Appraisal and (Internal and External) Failure Costs
QC	Quality Cost
RFQ	Request for Quotation
TCO	Total Cost of Ownership
TUT	Tampere University of Technology

Preface

The Cost Management Center (CMC) was established in 1998 with the idea of combining academic research with producing practically useful outputs for companies. Today, about ten years later, CMC is a well integrated part of the Department of Industrial Management in Tampere University of Technology. Since its establishment, CMC has constantly employed about ten full-time researchers focusing on research in various domains of management accounting. Throughout the existence of CMC, all its research projects have emphasised the learning opportunities that deep involvement in the development of management accounting practices in business organisations has to offer. In a sense, thanks to our engineering background, we have attempted to bring the collaborative and practice-oriented research practices common in many engineering fields to management accounting academia.

In this venture, the discussion around interventionist research, largely facilitated by Management Accounting Professor *Kari Lukka* from Turku School of Economics, has highlighted some very interesting methodological considerations with clear connections to the way we have been doing research. One of our first attempts at taking part in that methodological discussion with our empirical material was a conference paper presented in 2006 in the 6th New Directions in Management Accounting Conference co-chaired by Professor Lukka. After the conference, Professor Lukka encouraged us to take part in the CIMA Interventionist Research Initiative supporting interventionist management accounting research. We applied for funding, which led to discussions with Professor *Falconer Mitchell* from CIMA's Research and Development Group, and eventually we ended up packaging our experience in the form of this book.

During the past ten years, it has been interesting to monitor discussion on the pragmatic relevance of management accounting research and ways to enhance it. In addition, it has been highly motivating to take part in that discussion, even if this has still been from the margins. Thus, we would like to thank the two above-mentioned scholars for providing encouragement and supporting us in this venture, as well as CIMA for providing us with the funding for the writing process. We would also like to acknowledge the financial support provided by Tekes (the Finnish Funding Agency for Technology and Innovation) and the Academy of Finland. Furthermore, we wish to thank the managers of the numerous companies who not only have provided us with access to interesting research settings but also have shared part of the financial burden. Finally, we wish to express our gratitude to all our colleagues who have, at some point in time, participated in these research projects, hence providing the rich and interesting data that are used as starting points for this book.

Petri and Jouni
Tampere, November 2009

Introduction

This book sets out to contribute to discussion of the potential of the interventionist approach in management accounting (MA) research. Interventionist (IV) research has been suggested as a possibility for achieving contributions that have both theoretical and pragmatic relevance. The idea in this book is to draw on retrospective analysis to exploit interventionist research projects that have been conducted as sources of data. A set of interventionist studies is elaborated in order to address the potential benefits and advantages of the approach, as well as its potential risks and disadvantages. The main findings are outlined below.

POTENTIAL BENEFITS AND ADVANTAGES

Analysed studies demonstrated the potential versatility of the interventionist approach and some related advantages in management accounting research:

- Interventions may facilitate studies focusing on the practical meanings and impacts of relatively new MA technologies that are not yet widely diffused to companies.
- The idea of the intervening researcher may help in getting and building access to practice at different organisational levels, and the empirical research process can serve as a vehicle for explicating things that are perceived as invisible or non-discussable.
- Interventionist research can be seen as a wider programme that inherently addresses the practical utility of academic research and supports collaboration between academia and industry.
- Interventionist research is a part of researcher's toolbox: during the life cycle of a topic, IV research may shed light on emerging issues but may also be helpful in conducting 'reality-checks' in parallel to large-scale quantitative studies and experimental designs.
- Many kinds of intervention (including those outside management accounting) may catalyst management accounting considerations within organisations and thus create fruitful opportunities for

understanding the roles and meanings of management accounting in real environments.

POTENTIAL RISKS AND DISADVANTAGES

Our analysis also shows that interventionist research contains some risks and potential disadvantages:

- The extensive length of typical research processes connected with uncertainty about the explicit academic outcomes (publications) is a clear risk. In our experience, a typical interventionist project may last for two to six years.
- Theoretical contributions do not always stem from individual projects but from a series of them: the visibility of the theoretical value of empirical material is limited prior to the actual interventionist project.
- Strong managers and weak researchers form a vulnerable combination. Researchers have to be able to recognise their own aims and work for them, otherwise the results may place an unbalanced emphasis on practically relevant issues at the cost of academically interesting results.
- Conducting interventionist research calls for many qualities and abilities: succeeding in the empirical part requires an ability to naturally interact with the managers, while deriving academically acceptable output from the process requires good analytical skills, versatility and, to some extent, a multi-disciplinary knowledge base.
- Strong interventions contain a risk of creating highly idiosyncratic or even unrealistic settings ('synthetic anomalies'), which would not have been encountered without interventions.

Part I

Ten Years of Interventionist Research

1 Relevance Still Lost?

It has been claimed that management accounting research has failed to produce theories with pragmatic implications (see e.g. Hopwood 1983; Kaplan 1984; Kaplan 1986; Johnson and Kaplan 1987; Inanga and Schneider 2005). However, management accounting is an applied science (Kasanen et al. 1993), the idea of which is to produce theoretically grounded solutions for practical purposes (Mattessich 1995; see also Labro and Tuomela 2003).

Attempts have been made to overcome the problems of the pragmatic relevance of management accounting research by stressing the potential of in-depth empirical inquiries. Thus, case studies and field research have been seen as solutions to the problem (Kaplan 1984; Kaplan 1986). Yin (1994, p. 54) defines 'case study' as an empirical inquiry that investigates a contemporary phenomenon within its real-life context, addresses a situation in which the boundaries between the phenomenon and context are not clearly evident, and uses multiple sources of evidence. Case studies are considered useful when the phenomenon is complex, the theoretical base is thin, the phenomenon is difficult to study outside its natural environment (Bonoma 1985), or the different variables related to the phenomenon are not well-known (Meridith and Roth 1998). Furthermore, the case study approach is considered useful for discovering and describing new territories in the early phases of the theory-building process (Handfield and Melnyk 1998).

Although field research gained popularity among management accounting researchers in the 1980s (Ferreira and Merchant 1992), management accounting research has still suffered from its lack of connection to the practitioners' world. There remains an ongoing academic debate about what management accounting research is or should be (Zimmerman 2001; Hopwood 2002; Ittner and Larcker 2002; Luft and Shields 2002; Lukka and Mouritsen 2002). Some discussion on how to increase the relevance of management accounting can be found in the literature (see e.g. Kaplan 1984; Kaplan 1986; Zimmerman 2001; Inanga and Schneider 2005; Malmi and Granlund 2009). However, the general opinion among management accounting researchers still seems to be that management accounting research has failed to produce theories with such pragmatic implications. Thus, despite vivid academic debate on the issue, many scholars believe that the situation has not changed.

INTERVENTIONIST MANAGEMENT ACCOUNTING RESEARCH

In addition to case studies, interventionist research (Jönsson and Lukka 2007) has been suggested as one possible way to produce practically relevant management accounting research (Malmi and Granlund 2009). Interventionist research should be viewed as one form of case study, in which the researcher is deeply and actively involved with the object of study (Jönsson and Lukka 2007). In interventionist research, active participation in the field is regarded an asset rather than a liability. In other words, a good access to an empirical setting trough active participation is seen as more valuable than the risk of compromising objectivity.

However, despite the potential to produce a practically relevant contribution, the number of published interventionist studies in the area of management accounting is rather limited (Labro and Tuomela 2003). The small number of published interventionist studies (Seal et al. 1999; Tuomela 2005) has left researchers without guidance on how to conduct this type of research (Labro and Tuomela 2003). Thus, some additional examples of interventionist studies will enable researchers to better recognise how they have actually produced their theoretical contribution and what their pragmatic value has been. Furthermore, discussion is also needed on what actually can and should be seen as research intervention in interventionist management accounting research.

Professors Jönsson and Lukka (2007) have been important spokespeople for interventionist research and lately many other well-established scholars have also started to see it as an interesting opportunity to provide scientific contributions. Interestingly, even though many scholars have started to promote this research approach, it is rather unclear how common such research actually is. Most likely many research projects contain some interventionist characteristics in them but they are not reported as interventionist management accounting studies. As a result, instead of *ex-post* analyses of real-life interventionist studies, the potential advantages and disadvantages of the research approach are discussed more at the conceptual level. Therefore, there is a need for studies based on real-life interventionist research projects to provide empirical grounds for the academic discussions on the potential advantages and disadvantages of this research approach. In particular, more discussion is needed on the potential scope and intensity of research interventions.

INTERVENTIONIST RESEARCH—WHY STUDY IT IN FINLAND?

As was stated above, there is need for empirically based discussion on the nature and characteristics of interventionist management accounting research. In addition, is there perhaps a reason why the important spokespersons both come from Scandinavia (Professor Lukka from Finland and Professor

Jönsson from Sweden). When looking deeper into the research environment, the principles of research funding in Finland constitute an interesting contextual variable in relation to the interventionist research approach

Overall, Finland is a very research-intensive country, with research expenditures of approximately 3.5 percent of GDP. During the last ten years, Finland has been among the most active OECD countries with respect to research and development. There are a number of governmentally funded national organisations which provide support for universities and other research institutes. These include Tekes (the Finnish Funding Agency for Technology and Innovation), the Academy of Finland, and Sitra (the Finnish Innovation Fund). Each of these bodies not only provides funding for basic research and technology development but also supports more business-oriented research activities. During recent years, all three organisations have also funded research projects that touch the applications of management accounting. Especially, in the case of Tekes, industrial partners are considered essential; according to the policy of Tekes (Tekes 2009, www.tekes.fi):

> The key to success is a long-term commitment and co-operation between companies, researchers and funding organisations such as Tekes.

In operational terms this means that Tekes requires company participation in the research projects it provides funding for.

Companies that participate in research activities funded by Tekes do not only invest their time in the project but also cover a portion of the expenses arising from the research. Thus when companies engage in such research projects, they experience direct and negative cash flows and, as a result, they typically expect a fair payback from their investment. In other words, research has to be translated into something that is seen as valuable by them. While some companies might value collaboration with universities in itself, it is also possible that some of the expectations attached to joint research ventures are more direct and measurable in their nature. In our experience, it is far more feasible to attract companies into research participation when they can recognise, in addition to the public utility of investing in research, a more short-term utility connected with the research project. This is especially the case with small- and medium-sized companies which have limited investment capacity.

In all, this means that the Finnish innovation funding structure is, in our view, well in line with the idea of interventionist research. Companies are typically expecting active interventions by the researchers and, at the same time, are willing to make a serious commitment to the aims of the research. Thus the funding structure has facilitated both access to companies and collaboration with managers—even for management accounting researchers. However, there is also a downside to active management collaboration. Because companies provide partial funding and managers are involved day-to-day in the research projects, they have a tendency to actively steer the focus of these projects. Quite naturally, it is a crucial responsibility of the researchers to select and co-ordinate the participating companies in a manner that secures the scientific aims of these inquiries.

COST MANAGEMENT CENTER—HISTORY AND OBJECTIVES

Cost Management Center (CMC) is a research team at Tampere University of Technology (Finland) focusing on cost management and management accounting research. During the past ten years, CMC has completed over thirty long-term research projects with clear interventionist elements in them. All these research projects have been conducted with industrial partners, and researchers have been actively involved in the development of cost management and/or management reporting practices. The deep involvement of researchers in these development processes has provided a 'ringside seat' to observe them and contribute to the scientific community. Based on these research projects, over twenty refereed articles and more than 150 research papers have been published.

As was already pointed out, the funding structure of universities in Finland has some unique characteristics. In addition, especially in the case of universities of technology, the funding structure is very much driven by the National Funding Agency for Technology and Innovation (Tekes). Thus, engineering fields have a strong tradition of close industry–university collaboration and, since the beginning of CMC, one core idea has been to introduce engineering-style research to the management accounting world as well. As is typical of engineering research projects, all the projects conducted by CMC have included at least some interventionist elements in them. However, in addition to the interventionist elements, these projects have also included interview studies and even survey studies.

The funding structure has made CMC very industry-focused, especially compared with management accounting scholars in many other countries. Thus CMC seeks to improve the competitiveness of companies using the means of management accounting. This, naturally, means strong emphasis on field study with selected industrial partners. Because CMC seeks to help companies increase their competitiveness with the means and tools of management accounting, one aim is to study various contemporary trends and to connect them with management accounting. Thus the research work in CMC is not so much about accounting *per se* but rather how to apply accounting tools and principles in the changing business environment. Some topics under investigation include the following:

- Changes in the earnings models
- Supporting R&D decisions with cost and profitability information
- Cost management in global business (supply) networks

- Life cycle costing
- Cost implications of mass customisation and standardisation
- Ensuring cost efficiency in open innovations

To illustrate the approach, when looking at inter-organisational cost management, many of the existing cost management tools have simply been applied to a new accounting context. In other words, the cost management tools are by and large the same (target costing, ABC . . .), but instead of one company, two or more companies are involved. However, when carefully studied, the context itself might not be that unique either. In their research project, Laine et al. (2006), for example, have identified some conceptual similarities between manufacturing networks and consolidated companies which have provided an interesting analogy for analysing costs and profits in manufacturing networks. Such a project is a nice example of how appropriate analogies and metaphors developed by management accounting researchers are able to help managers and fellow researchers to cope with phenomena that might appear to be something unique, especially at first glance.

OBJECTIVE OF THE BOOK

Our intention is to contribute to the discussion of the potential of the interventionist approach when trying to produce contributions associated with both theoretical and pragmatic relevance. The idea is to use the ten years of CMC's practical experience in doing interventionist research as a source of data. A selection of past research processes is elaborated in order to address the advantages as well as the potential risks and disadvantages of the approach.

The intended audience for this book can be divided in two. On the one hand, this book will contribute to academic discussion of the potential of the interventionist research approach and, thus, a key audience will be fellow researchers. On the other hand, the book will provide new aspects and perspectives to the practitioners who are planning to become engaged in interventionist research projects with academics. Despite the importance of practitioners in interventionist research, their needs and perspectives have not been extensively discussed in the existing literature on interventionist research.

This book largely builds on the work by Jönsson and Lukka (2007) and tries to continue a dialogue on different approaches to interventionist management accounting research. The main objective is to discuss the scope and intensity of possible research interventions in management accounting research. However, instead of just conceptual discussion, this book (1) provides an *ex-post* analysis of a number of research projects conducted by CMC, illustrating the potential variety of research interventions in management accounting research, both in terms of scope and intensity. In addition, the book also (2) aims at classifying the different types of research intervention thus far experienced in the research projects of CMC. Hence it forms a basis for a more structured and eventually normative approach to research interventions in the management accounting domain. In addition to the *ex-post* analysis of conducted research projects, this book also (3) provides empirical evidence on managers' perspectives on interventionist research and its potential in ensuring pragmatic relevance of the research results. The most important industry participants of the research projects analysed in this book are interviewed in order to reflect the process of interventionist research from the practitioners' point of view.

The book consists of three parts and is organised as follows. Part I will briefly introduce the idea of interventionist research based on the extant literature. In addition, Part I also discusses the framework developed for analysing the scope and intensity of research interventions. Part II will provide—for those that are more interested in hands-on evidence—numerous empirical examples of interventionist research projects together with analysis of their theoretical and pragmatic implications within the domain of management accounting. In Part III, conclusions and lessons learned are presented—addressing not only the potential of interventionist research but also its evident risks. As there is always at least two groups of stakeholders involved in interventionist research, both the researchers' and the practitioners' perspectives on potential and risks are discussed. In all, the book seeks to communicate that management accounting research should not be something disconnected from the problems of real-life managers and management accountants. On the contrary, professional accountants and other practitioners—for us this refers to people that run businesses—should be aware of the potential that interventionist research projects can offer them.

2 Interventionist Research in Brief

> *Researchers* [in accounting] *need to ask practitioners and users questions about issues of importance to them.* (Inaga and Schneider 2005, p. 246)

In the pursuit of sound management accounting theory and theory contribution—which can be seen as inherent qualities of any management accounting research agenda—the key concept of theory has recently evoked an important debate. Malmi and Granlund (2009) are concerned with the ability of the extant theories in MA to provide support for practitioners. In all, Malmi and Granlund subscribe to the applied nature of the discipline and argue that management accounting theory, in its different forms, should be usable for creating valuable MA practices (see also Ittner and Larcker 2002). That is, the management accounting research community should fully acknowledge its primary customers: real-life organisations that might benefit from accounting tools, techniques and practices. Unfortunately, this has not sufficiently been the case historically, resulting in the lack of substance in accounting research that is of practical value (cf. Inaga and Schneider 2005).

What has been suggested for resolving the problem? In addition to a number of suggestions that relate to traditional empirical inquiry and theoretical frames of reference (see Malmi and Granlund [2009]; Inanga and Schneider [2005] for a more complete discussion) as well as methodological heterogeneity in general (Lukka and Mouritsen 2002), investments in interventionist work, in particular, have been welcomed.

WHAT IS INTERVENTIONIST RESEARCH?

Interventionist research (Jönsson and Lukka 2007) has been suggested as one possible way to produce practically relevant management accounting research (Malmi and Granlund 2009). However, what makes interventionist research different from case studies, and what is research intervention? Empirical case studies utilise interviews and observation as the main data gathering methods (Jönsson and Lukka 2007), whereas interventionist research views the researcher as a facilitator of change. Thus, instead of simply being an observer, the researcher is actively trying to exert an influence on the organisation under observation, i.e. to intervene. In other words, the researcher in interventionist research is an active—intervening—participant in the case organisation (Tuomela 2005).

The idea of research interventions can be closely related to cultural change interventions (Schein 1999), which focus, for example, on issues of concern to top managers (primary interventions) or the stories and legends told (secondary interventions) in order to facilitate certain cultural change within an organisation. However, in interventionist research, instead of studying the interventions of managers, the researchers themselves actually intervene in order to facilitate a certain change process and use this learning process as a means to provide theoretical contribution.

Jönsson and Lukka (2007) provide a good overview of the characteristics and methodological justifications of interventionist research, which shall not be discussed here in more detail. Interventionist research should be viewed as one form of case study, in which the researcher is deeply and actively involved with the object of study (Jönsson and Lukka 2007). In the same way as case study itself, interventionist research forms a cluster of research approaches, which most notably include the following research traditions:

- Action research (originating in the work of Lewin [1946]) in the field of social sciences)
- Action science (a stream of interventionist research suggested by Argyris et al. [1985])
- Design science (introduced by van Aken [2004])
- Clinical research (see, e.g., Normann [1976] in Jönsson and Lukka [2005])
- Constructive research (see, e.g., Kasanen et al. [1993]; Lukka [2000]; Labro and Tuomela [2003])
- Innovation action research (Kaplan [1998])
- Conditional-normative research approach (Mattessich [1995])

These alternative forms of interventionist research differ, for example, in the importance they attach to the practical and theoretical views of the study as well as in the extent of the researcher's intervention.

The following arguments quite directly supporting the interventionist approach can be found in the literature:

- More emphasis on context: to be relevant, or to increase its relevance and substance value, accounting research has to be aligned with specific contexts, bearing in mind the appropriate interrelationships and interdependencies present. Specifically, Inaga and Schneider (2005) perceive accounting as a communication activity, implying considerations that focus both on its information content based on real needs (the core of communication) and its formulation or packaging of that content (Inaga and Schneider 2005).
- More emphasis on the studies with the constructive research approach where the researchers actively participate in the innovation process of new *management control*[1] constructs. An important rationale for

this is based on an idea that the validity of the results—that is refined theory—is weighted through real-life implementation. As Malmi and Granlund (2009) put it: "what works in practice is true".

- More effort in "opening the black boxes of organisation", meaning that the research community is not as aware of conditions and realities in companies and other users of accounting practices as it ought to be (Jönsson and Lukka 2007).

Jönsson and Lukka (2007) suggest that the association between interventionist research and case studies in general is quite close. However, they stress that, in principle, interventionists can also engage in methodological approaches other than case studies. When it comes to management accounting, the extant literature—published for instance in *Accounting, Organisations and Society, European Accounting Review,* or *Management Accounting Research*—includes a body of case-based research, offering insights into the practices of accounting in different organisational contexts. Most of the published pieces belonging to this body can be characterised as interpretive—or subjective, bearing in mind that the borderline between objective and subjective research is not necessarily clear cut (see Kakkuri-Knuuttila et al. 2008a, b; Ahrens 2008). Given these two generalisations—interventionist studies are cases and cases are interpretive—one might easily conclude that interventionist research in MA is necessarily interpretive. This would be too straightforward a conclusion however. Just as we can identify objective and subjective genres in non-interventionist empirical research, we can also identify the *possibility* of objective and subjective types of interventionist work. Discussion of the differences and similarities between these two is beyond the scope of this book, but even acknowledgement of these alternative types at the general level reminds us of the potential and versatile applications of interventionist research.

SUGGESTIONS FOR CONDUCTING INTERVENTIONIST WORK

Labro and Tuomela (2003) have analysed two empirical studies that closely resemble the constructive research approach suggested by Kasanen et al. (1993). On the basis of their analysis, they have provided a number of methodological suggestions for conducting this type of empirical research. Constructive research being related to the notion of interventionist research (see Jönsson and Lukka 2007), we feel that it is also important to consider the suggestions of Labro and Tuomela at this instance:

- Critical success factors in the preparatory phase before entering into the actual project are:
  - To assure commitment and enthusiasm—not only from researcher(s) but also from several company members

- To check the availability of sufficient resources
- To confirm consistency between managers' and researchers' values
- To invest in managerial understanding of the features and logic of the research approach
- To make an agreement on the publication of results
- Teamwork during the empirical phase of the study is important not only for gaining acceptance for the developed construct but also for securing the interpretive results of the study.
- The possibility of different kinds of theoretical contributions should be acknowledged. More objective contributions may relate to the introduction of novel constructs as such, whereas what might be called interpretive contributions circle around or are grounded in those constructs.
- Active effort for the implementation of constructs is an essential part of interventionist work—leading either to successful application or rejection. We can learn from both cases.

While the efforts of Tuomela and Labro (2003) are notable in clarifying the methodological concerns *predominantly within the research process* in constructive research or interventionist research, it seems that more discussion is needed to reach an understanding of a number of further issues that also partly touch broader concerns (which lie outside the process of a specific study):

- Are there situations in which interventionist research is particularly useful?
- Given the cross-disciplinary nature of management accounting in real-life, how can we position and focus interventionist research in MA. What are the variants of interventionist research and what purpose might they serve?
- What are the requirements that interventionist research poses to a researcher?

As opposed to consultancy, interventionist research—despite its normative or prescriptive purposes—is strongly theoretically connected (Jönsson and Lukka 2007). As put by Ahrens and Chapman (2006), p. 820: "With qualitative methodology goes an acknowledgment that the field is itself not just part of the empirical world but is shaped by the theoretical interests of the researcher." Field selection is not the same as research question or paradigm selection. This applies to interventionist work as well—even at the level of intervention. Independently of the target of intervention, research questions might be informed by theoretical frames that go beyond the surface of intervention.

RATIONALE FOR INTERVENTIONIST APPROACH

As pointed out by current literature (see Ahrens and Chapman 2007; Mouritsen et al. 2009), management accounting and management control systems both affect and are affected by organisational norms and values. While the above notion, as such, has been elaborated to some extent within the interpretive management accounting research that has been conducted in different contexts, it has mainly been mobilised in research agendas by *observing* the accounting practices in place (cf. Burchell et al. 1985; March 1987; Ahrens and Chapman 2007). Despite the indisputable merit of this line of research, it is important to realise the added-value of interventionist research in this respect. While the studies with observation-based data gathering have to limit themselves to interpreting management accounting and control practices that have already been implemented, this limitation does not necessarily concern interventionist studies. It has been shown by a substantial amount of empirical research that there are many constructs in management accounting which are not especially widely implemented by real-life organisations (consider, for instance, throughput accounting, open-book accounting, life cycle costing or even ABC). Interventionist research can engage in the implementation processes of new (or old but modestly diffused) MA constructs and thus provide valuable empirical insights into the interdependency between novel accounting approaches and organisational values or norms. In other words, especially with regard to possible new theoretical ideas in management accounting, interventionist research can increase the efficiency of the process of empirical validation by reducing the lead-time from idea to implementation.

Vollmer (2009) argues that management accounting has become a "normal social science" that hosts a number of competing paradigms and is associated with pluralism of approaches (see also Ahrens et al. 2008). This state of affairs is seen as promising, thus offering its scholars with many possibilities: " . . . *normal social science in management accounting as anywhere else offers its scholars and students plentiful opportunities to marvel at, exploit, replenish and reopen the cracks within social life and across its academic and everyday discourses*" (Vollmer 2009, p. 149).

3   A Framework For Analysing Interventions

As was pointed out in Chapter 1, this book largely builds on the work by Jönsson and Lukka (2007) and tries to continue the debate about different approaches to interventionist management accounting research. However, instead of conceptual discussion, this book provides an *ex-post* analysis of some research projects conducted by CMC. This chapter begins with an introduction to the way of doing research in CMC and before going in to the actual cases in Part II, the framework used for analysing the selected research projects will be introduced.

FROM INDIVIDUALS TO TEAMS AND PROJECTS TO A RESEARCH PORTFOLIO

In CMC, the research is organised in projects but the ultimate aim is to utilise the accumulated competencies of the whole research team. Thus, instead of individuals, the importance of the research team is highlighted. Based on our experience, the existence of the research team provides some interesting insights into how to carry out research.

First, the research team provides access to different types of competency that can be harnessed in different projects when needed. For example, some projects might require a cost model to be built at the beginning, and the team can provide capabilities for that. After the company understands, for example, customer profitability in more detail (based on the new costing model), some other researchers may continue the project with the aim of intervening in the development of sales processes in order to improve the profitability of not-so-profitable customers. In this, some competencies related to product development might be needed and that knowledge can be provided by a third CMC member. In fact, the research team and its accumulated knowledge have turned out to be a valuable resource when accessing companies with new research projects. This is rather different from contemporary management accounting research where researchers tend to collaborate mainly in the writing phase of the study, and not that extensively in the empirical phase. Rather than the management accounting world, the approach of CMC is closer to the world of medical research, where large teams are used to investigate a certain issue and publications have large numbers of names in them as a result of many people having contributed to the research process with their speciality knowledge.

Secondly, the accumulated experience in research projects creates not only a collection of research projects and case studies but rather a set of 'research streams' with lots of empirical data. For example, one of the first projects of CMC focused on cost management practices in product development (the Rapid Research Project) and it included three case companies. The first one, Kalmar Oy, manufactures container handling equipment used, for example, in harbours. The research work in Kalmar Oy focused on analysing the manufacturing costs of a certain pilot product. The second one, Metso Minerals, manufactures mining equipment and the case study focused on different types of customer-specific changes in product specifications while the cost analyses focused more on the effects of customisation on the spare part business. The third company in the Rapid Research Project was Sandvik Mining and Construction, where the research work focused on component standardisation and its potential cost implications. These case studies are shown in Figure 3.1.

In all three companies, the researchers were responsible for providing new kinds of cost information to the decision makers. In other words, the creation of new cost reports can be seen as the primary research intervention. However, when looking at the broader perspective, the project gave CMC its first touch on mass customisation—customisation and component standardisation are both important elements connected by the mass customisation framework. The interventionist work done for Metso Minerals Oy was an important starting point for the first dissertation focusing on mass customisation written in CMC (Sievänen 2004).

At the same time as the Rapid Research Project ended, a new research partner was found. In the autumn of 2000, CMC had engaged in a research project focusing on modularisation of conveyor systems for the food industry with Antti Lindfors Oy. In that case, the research interventions focused on cost management by developing new product solutions

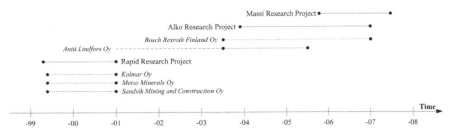

Figure 3.1   Interventionist research projects focusing on mass customisation and its cost implications.

and analysing their potential cost effects. The solutions in that study provided interesting insights for another company, and that was the starting point for the Alko Research Project focusing on mass customisation and component commonality in the engineering-to-order (ETO) context. This work then evolved into a larger research project focusing on mass customisation (the Massi Research Project). However, in this project, the number of companies involved was significantly higher and, as a result, the role of research interventions was not that significant. Nevertheless, in order to gather data, researchers still spent significant amounts of time helping the companies participating in the Massi Research Project. In all these projects, different individual researchers have been used based on their speciality competencies.

Finally, in addition to recognising the importance of the research team, it is interesting to point out the long time-frame that has been needed to learn how to carry out interventionist research with companies. Perhaps now, after ten years and thirty research projects, there is enough accumulated experience to discuss the challenges and the potential of interventionist management accounting research. However, many more experiences and interventionist research projects are needed to make the method part of mainstream management accounting research. Our next challenges will be to start publishing the results in management accounting journals (most of the refereed articles, thus far, have been published in other journals) and to promote the potential of interventionist research as a tool to bring practitioners and management accounting scholars closer to each other.

SIX RESEARCH STREAMS SELECTED

Chapter 1 introduced some examples of topics or 'research streams' that are currently under investigation at CMC. This book is based on *ex-post* analysis on six of CMC's research streams in order to understand the scope and intensity of possible research interventions by management accounting researchers aiming at contributing to the management accounting literature. The main research streams are shown in Figure 3.2.

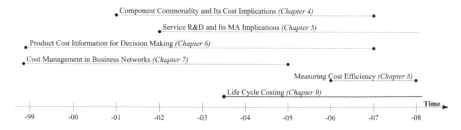

Figure 3.2   The research streams of CMC analysed in this research report.

This sample of research streams only contains a small part of the research projects conducted by CMC. These projects have been selected in order to illustrate the different types of research interventions thus far identified by CMC's researchers. Thus, even within CMC's projects, some other types of research intervention could, most likely, be found. Some of the research streams shown above contain several research projects (i.e., there is a continuum of research projects), with each project involving two or more case companies. Others, on the other hand, include long-term collaboration only with one case company.

Furthermore, all research streams discussed in this book contain research interventions but the scope and intensity of these research interventions vary from case to case, thus providing some empirical data on possible research interventions in interventionist management accounting research. In addition, the time lines shown in Figure 3.2 merely illustrate the time span of the research collaboration discussed in this report. Even if the research work in some research streams seems to have ended, research work on all these six areas is still carried on either conceptually (in the form of academic publications) or empirically. However, that work is not used as empirical material in this book.

ANALYSING THE STRENGTH OF RESEARCH INTERVENTIONS

Despite the scarcity of empirical examples (see Jönsson and Lukka 2007), it has been argued that the domain of interventionist studies may be divided into a number of variants that differ from each other, for example in terms of the researcher's role or the strength of intervention (cf. Westin and Roberts 2007). As a classification criterion, Jönsson and Lukka (2007) distinguish between studies that work through strong and modest interventions. Strong interventions aim at changing the processes of the host organisation by re-engineering the control system related to those processes, or by suggesting alternative designs for the processes themselves. On the contrary, modest interventions are less intrusive and active—they primarily serve as facilitators or catalysts for change.

For the purpose of our *ex-post* analysis, we develop a more refined measure of intervention strength, which builds on the idea of modest and strong interventions presented by Jönsson and Lukka (2007). We use a scale from Level 1 to Level 5 for describing the strength of intervention. On this scale, Level 1 corresponds to modest intervention where the mere presence of the researcher(s) facilitates the change or novel thinking. Active participation by the researchers is very limited, and they may be seen as external resources or capacity with a symbolic value. As an example, the presence of a well-known cost accounting expert in a product development project meeting would serve as a symbolic (interventionist) act that would most likely highlight the importance of cost consideration in the development project. Level 2 refers to the types of intervention that rely on external expertise imported into the organisation by the researchers. The expertise is, however, employed in a manner that resembles the 'modest' category in Jönsson and Lukka (2007). Actual interaction or participation is thus limited, which means that the researcher remains an outsider rather than an insider for most of the time so has an *etic* or outsider rather than an *emic* or insider perspective (see Jönsson and Lukka 2007 for discussion of the dynamism related to *emic/etic* perspectives). As an example, the implementation of specific accounting techniques (like open-book accounting or target costing) may benefit from the import of expertise, which in turn facilitates the researcher's aim of observing, say, the consequences of the implementation within the given organisational setting.

The middle of our scale, Level 3, already has some of the features of strong intervention. We refer to studies that are characterised by rich and active participation in real development projects or considerations but that clearly have a limited organisational coverage. For most of the organisation, the researcher is predominantly an outsider. This is most often the case, especially in large international organisations which engage in interventionist research. The intervention may remain at a local or at a functional level, and the resulting ideas or awareness of the process do not get widely diffused into the rest of organisation. We acknowledge that this interpretation is, however, largely tied up with the question of the unit of analysis of the study. For example, if the intervention is about coping with some idiosyncrasies related to, say, Finnish culture, the result may not even have potential for wider international employment. Thus, local intervention based on the active input of researchers is about as strong as it can get in this respect.

The strong end of our scale includes Levels 4 and 5. With Level 4, we refer to studies that in many respects seek to make strong interventions—building new and practically meaningful constructions, suggesting and arguing for new ways to operate, introducing new organisational paradigms etc.—but that nevertheless do not reach the extreme end of emic or insider status. The intervening researcher may be seen as 'almost family' but he or she still lacks the image of the true insider, which means that some of the most silent values or rules of authority may remain invisible. As a result, the researcher cannot really 'suffer the culture' (see Jönssön and Lukka 2005 citing Hastrup 1997). This should not necessarily be seen as a handicap but it is an important aspect to acknowledge at least in the reflection phase of the study. Finally, Level 5 refers to those—perhaps extremely rare—studies that make strong interventions on the basis of active input by researchers and that typically are associated with a long-term (for example, 3–6 year) commitment that allows a researcher's true immigration to emic, insider status. In other words, the researcher becomes 'one of us' for most of the people in the organisation—having rights and responsibilities resembling that of an employee while not being, for example, an employee who is working for his/her PhD.

FOCAL POINT OF RESEARCH INTERVENTION

In addition to intervention strength, we also adopted a classification based on the focal point of the intervention. By this, we refer to how far the researcher is directly intervening in management accounting (MA) practices or tools within this discipline and how far the focus of intervention touches other disciplines, such as engineering or marketing. This kind of classification has not been explicitly present in the extant literature but nevertheless we perceive it as important and interesting, especially when taking into account the applied nature of management accounting (see Labro and Tuomela 2003). Management accounting mirrors or translates (cf. Mouritsen et al. 2009) activities in the real processes of organisations, meaning that whatever happens in an organisation, there will be—or there could be—a management accounting perspective on it. This perspective can take the form of a single calculus, a set of financial scenarios, a conceptual framework or a number of other representations generally aimed at better control over events. As Malmi and Granlund (2009) aptly point out:

> [W]e are claiming that MA theory should be a set of propositions of how to organize accounting and control practices under given circumstances.

To us, this implies that interventions aimed at MA contribution do not always have to focus on accounting itself. On the contrary, it is also possible and sometimes justified to set out interventions aimed at creating certain—as phrased by Malmi and Granlund—*circumstances* which are seen as interesting in relation to management accounting controls.

Again, a scale of Level 1 to 5 is employed in positioning the studies with respect to MA focus. Starting from the more traditional end, Level 5 refers to studies focusing on management accounting constructs and practices as focal points of intervention. As an example, Tuomela (2005) aimed at introducing a new kind of performance measurement application—a so-called Customer Scorecard—into an organisation. Level 4 studies would also focus on MA constructs, but while strongly supporting the ideas bubbling in the MA domain they would be interested as well in making a difference within other disciplines. As an example, a researcher wishing to introduce a new means of cost control in sourcing could be interested also in making an intervention in the processes of sourcing management in order to secure a better correspondence between the intended controls and the context of control. Levels 3 and 2 represent the next steps in this continuum, reflecting different emphases between MA and other disciplines.

Finally, the seemingly rebellious flavour of Level 1 study deserves a short elaboration. What do we mean by saying that the focus 'is solely on other disciplines' than MA? It goes without saying that research aimed at contributing to management accounting has to have a connection with MA; however, we suggest that it is possible to enter an organisation without an intention to intervene in management accounting and still make a management accounting contribution. This necessitates observation (or data collection more generally) and reflection that are focused on issues that are relevant to MA. In other words, the question is about the focal point of the *intervention* not the focal point of the study as a whole.

FRAMEWORK FOR ANALYSING THE SELECTED RESEARCH STREAMS

The two dimensions discussed in the previous sections—strength and focal point of interventions—provide a framework (see Figure 3.3) that is then

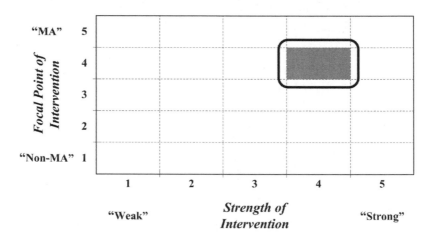

Key	Strength	Focal point (of access)
5	Strong collaboration, native role 'one of us'	Intervention solely on MA practices/tools
4	Active and versatile participation, 'almost family'	Intervention mainly on MA and partly other
3	Rich participation within limited domain	Equal focus on MA and other
2	External expert, limited participation	Main focus on other disciplines, also MA
1	Intervention through presence, very limited participation in processes	Focus solely on other disciplines

Figure 3.3   The framework used for analysing selected research projects.

used as a basis for analysing the selected research streams. Based on the subjective judgment of the authors, positioning conveys a message that the selected studies or research streams have different characteristics measured by these two variables. Although the selection does not fully satisfy the requirements of theoretical sampling (cf. Yin 1994), our portfolio of selected interventionist studies nevertheless gives a fair foundation for discussing the potential variants of the research approach.

In Part II of this book, these projects are discussed in more detail. Each chapter in Part starts with a short introduction positioning the case using the previously discussed framework. After that, the structure of each chapter is as follows. First, existing literature is briefly summarised showing explicitly the need for theoretical contribution to the substance area of the case study. Thus, the literature focuses on the management accounting domain that each case attempts to contribute to and not on the interventionist research method. Secondly, research objectives and the research setting are briefly discussed. The third part of each chapter focuses on theoretical contribution in the management accounting domain. It is worth noting that some cases may provide much more potential for theoretical contribution than is discussed here, but this book mainly discusses areas that have been published or are in the publication process so the theoretical contribution of each case can be better argued. Next, the managerial implications of each case are shown in order to illustrate the pragmatic relevance of each research project or research stream. Finally, each chapter concludes with a description of the research interventions, enabling interested readers to get some taste of the interventionist research world in practice.

Part II discusses each of the selected research streams in more detail. As was previously pointed out, the analysis framework used in this book

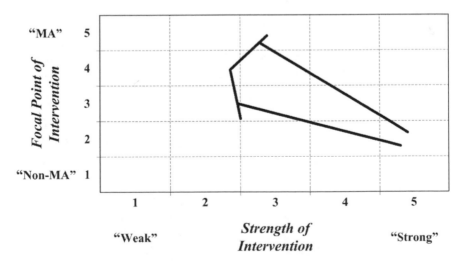

Figure 3.4 Cases discussed in Part II.

positions the research streams based on the strength and focal point of intervention. Part II has been organized in a way that the strength of the intervention diminishes case by case. This has been chosen in order to show first the elements more different from the existing discussion on the interventionist research methodology; in the end, the weaker interventions are not that far from mainstream research projects with ethnographic elements in them (in-depth case studies or action research).

It should be noted that this book has been written in such a way that Part II can be skipped in case the reader wishes just to study interventionist management accounting research at the more conceptual level. However, the analytical descriptions provided in Part II provide grounds for the empirical findings discussed in Part III. Furthermore, even though the structure of each chapter in Part II has been standardised in terms of titles, there can be some differences regarding the content. In each chapter, the main emphasis is on the themes that seem to add most clearly to the extant understanding of interventionist research—acknowledging the view of both researchers and practitioners. As a result, even though the titles are the same, the content of each section may be somewhat different from each other.

Part II

Selected Research Projects

4 Accessing Information at the Emic Level

As was pointed out in the conclusion of Part I, each chapter in Part II focuses on one interesting element in terms of interventionist management accounting research. This chapter starts the discussion by showing, perhaps, an extremely rare case where researchers were truly able to penetrate to the *emic* level. This chapter discusses a long-term research project focusing on the cost implications of component commonality. The research work within this area started in 2001, although the topic did not become relevant to the case company until 2003. Research collaboration with the case company had started already in 1999, but in a totally different area. Interestingly, the results achieved in the other company motivated this case company management to re-focus the on-going research project, showing the importance of the use of the cumulative learning gathered in various research projects as an asset to gain deep access to interesting research topics in organizations.

This chapter illustrates how research interventions and active participation in the development process help researchers reach the insider, *emic* level needed to understand the reality experienced by a business's managers. The interventions discussed in this chapter are classified in Figure 4.1.

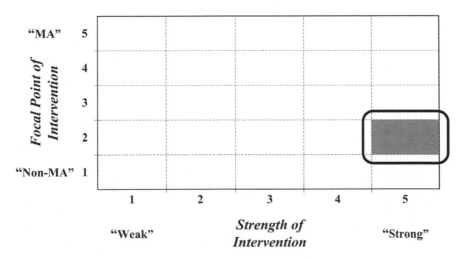

Figure 4.1 Scope and intensity of the research interventions within this case company.

As seen in Figure 4.1, this chapter shows research interventions that, on one hand, are very strong, but on the other hand, do not focus so much on the management accounting field. Instead, the focus is mainly on product and process development. In this case, the researchers really gained 'one of us' status inside the organisation and, despite the main focus on non-management accounting interventions, they were able to use that as a way to contribute to the existing theory on management accounting, especially in the area of component commonality and its potential cost implications.

COMPONENT COMMONALITY AND ITS COST IMPLICATIONS

Component commonality can be defined as the use of the same version of a component across multiple products (Labro 2004). Component commonality is usually seen as a means to increase product variety without sacrificing cost efficiency, or to achieve cost savings without sacrificing product variety. In the existing literature, component commonality is mainly increased by replacing product-specific components with a common component without any major changes in the product architecture. When component commonality is increased by replacing several product-specific components with a common one, the common component has to fulfil the functional requirements of several unique components (Hillier 2000, 2002; Krishnan and Gupta 2001; Fong et al. 2004; Zhou and Gruppström 2004). Thus, the common component often needs to be over-specified, which primarily means two things: the common component either has to include the functionality of several components and, in a sense, have unnecessary functions built into it (e.g., a car dashboard can have 'empty' places for switches needed only for different optional features) or it has to have capacity that exceeds the need associated with some of the end products (e.g., an electric drive has to be chosen based on the largest demand).

Labro (2003, later published in 2004) has made an extensive review of literature discussing component commonality and its potential cost implications. In her study, Labro concluded that the potential cost implications of component commonality are manifold and not yet completely understood. Despite this, the existing literature on component commonality emphasises four aspects related to cost management: (1) commonality indices, (2) cost of over-specification, (3) cost reductions in the costs of operations and (4) the use of transaction drivers in cost analyses. In order to later point out the theoretical contribution of this case, let us look at each of these four aspects in a bit more detail.

First, commonality indices form an essential part of the existing component commonality literature (for a summary, see Kaski 2002; Thevenot and Simpson 2006; Zwerink et al. 2007). Different indices have been proposed but the most traditional and most widely used commonality index is the Collier Index (see Collier 1981, 1982). The Collier Index, in short, sets out how many different components are needed for a certain product family. Thus, the smaller the number of components needed to offer a certain product variety, the better the commonality index value. Secondly, as pointed out, component commonality is typically implemented using over-specification which is often expected to result in higher costs. Interestingly, the idea that a common component replacing several product-specific components might actually be more expensive (often referred to as the cost of over-specification) did not emerge until the 1990s (Gerchak et al. 1988; Ulrich 1995; Eynan and Rosenblatt 1996). However, since then, the assumption regarding the cost of over-specification has become a rather dominant element in the literature. In addition, managers tend to recognise this too.

Thirdly, the component commonality literature focuses primarily on three organisational functions: manufacturing, materials management and product development (for a more detailed analysis, see Lyly-Yrjän-äinen 2008). With these activities, the number of components is seen as an important cost driver which, at the same time, is easy to measure. When interpreted this way, commonality easily becomes an optimisation exer-cise. The focus thus remains on using commonality as a means to optimise batch sizes, inventory levels and frequency of deliveries (driver rates used in cost analyses) rather than on exploiting the possible effects of commonality on the structures of business processes. The use of over-specification as a means to implement commonality also supports this interpretation.

Finally, because component commonality is mainly seen as having an impact on driver rates of different operational costs, it has been only natural to use transaction drivers for illustrating the potential cost implications of component commonality (see, for example, Thyssen et al. 2006). However, transaction drivers tend to include all transactions. Thus, reduction in the number of components is expected to result in the same cost implications regardless of what components are actually being reduced. Labro (2004) points out in her study that component commonality may also impact the cost rates (that is the unit costs) of many activities but the existing cost analyses, nevertheless, are primarily based on the use of transaction driv-ers. This could be because they are relatively easy to measure and use in cost simulations and the earlier-mentioned optimisation exercises.

RESEARCH OBJECTIVES AND RESEARCH SETTING

Interestingly, these four aspects seem to be closely related to the use of over-specification as a means of implementing component commonality. However, when looking at component commonality literature, there seems to be another factor supporting strongly the four aspects discussed above. Component commonality and its cost implications have been studied pri-marily in make-to-stock (MTS) and assembly-to-order (ATO) contexts (see Thomas 1992, Perera et al. 1999, Fong et al. 2004). The make-to-stock (MTS) context can be characterised as an environment in which production is scheduled according to forecast customer demand, and the actual demand is then met from the finished product inventory (Molina et al. 2007). In an assembly-to-order (ATO) context, it is only component production that is based on predicted sales volumes; the final products are assembled based on customer orders. In both contexts, there are explicitly defined product families, which make it easy to use over-specification as a means to implement commonality, and commonality indices to measure the impacts. Again, the use of over-specification supports these optimisation exercises, focusing on operative costs and use of transaction drivers in cost analyses.

However, the existing literature on component commonality and its cost implications does not explicitly address the possible connections between these contexts and the cost (management) implications of commonality, which is an important shortcoming considering the general consensus on component commonality and its potential cost implications. In addition to contextual considerations, the extant literature is lacking evidence on the effects of commonality in the engineering-to-order (ETO) context. *Thus, the objective of this case study is to discuss component commonality and its potential cost management implications in ETO contexts.*

The ETO context is typical for products that need unique engineering design or a significant amount of customisation in order to be manufactured according to customer-specific requirements (Amaro et al. 1999). Thus, each order results in a unique design, set of part numbers, bill of material, and routing (McGovern et al. 1999; Hicks and Braiden 2000; Hicks et al. 2001). Furthermore, in the ETO context, products are not configured using existing modules and product options, but rather the product (or at least part of it) is engineered individually for each customer. ETO strategy results in highly customised products but also, in many cases, in lengthy delivery times and high costs. ETO strategy is very common in various business-to-business (B2B) industries and hence should not be overlooked; capital goods are often customised by being engineered to order.

As an empirical basis, this chapter analyses an interventionist case study conducted in co-operation with a wholesaler of hydraulic components. The research project first focused on product profitability in the company's wholesaling activities. However, in addition to component sales, the company also manufactures hydraulic power units. In an effort to reduce costs and delivery times, the company had started to modularise its power units. The modularisation project had not progressed well enough however and, as a result, the Managing Director decided to engage the researchers in the development process as external resources. The researchers had been involved in similar projects before and in fact one of them had a patented solution enabling efficient customisation of conveyor systems manufactured with an ETO strategy (Patent No. 116130). Due to these synergies, at some point the research focus in the case company shifted from wholesale operations to power unit manufacturing, and the rest of that project was used as a 'pre-study' for a three-year-long research project focusing on component commonality in the ETO context. The main elements of the research collaboration are shown in Figure 4.2.

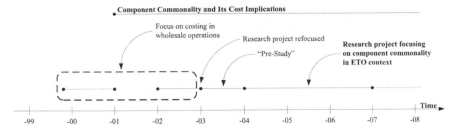

Figure 4.2 Timeline of the research collaboration with the case company.

The study presented in this chapter includes not only management account-ing interventions but also interventions targeted on product development and organisation of the supply chain. The researchers had excellent access to the collaborating firm in the insider, *emic* mode and there was a mutual under-standing between the researchers and the case company management that the researchers' interventions were part of this co-operation. These features not only made it possible for the researchers to develop the primary research project in a fruitful manner, but they also offered a good opportunity to reflect on the conducted study from various perspectives from the inside.

THEORETICAL CONTRIBUTION

When comparing the contextual characteristics of MTS and ATO contexts to the contextual characteristics of the ETO context, there are some clear differ-ences. First, instead of standardised products, the products in ETO contexts are customised and are sometimes very unique. Because the products are unique, explicitly defined product families do not exist. Secondly, the cust-omisation typical of the ETO approach means that production volumes at the component and product levels are relatively low, especially when compared to MTS and ATO contexts. Thirdly, the low component-level and product-level volumes combined with high demand uncertainty result in operations where components are manufactured and purchased only for customer proj-ects and hence only a very few components are or can be stored.

These differences in the contextual characteristics also mean that com-ponent commonality and its implications in the ETO context are rather different from those of MTS and ATO contexts and, as a result, the cost implications are also very different. In fact, the four aspects emphasised in the extant component commonality literature do not seem very valid in ETO contexts. Because there are no explicitly defined product families, (1) commonality indices are practically impossible to use and, for the very same reason, (2) over-specification alone no longer works as a way to increase component commonality. In the ETO context, component commonality is not used as a means to optimise logistics processes and manufacturing batches, but on the contrary, (3) it is used to reduce the costs of the project-management-related white-collar work. Finally, (4) easy-to-measure transaction drivers do not seem to capture the cost reduction potential that is embedded in the white-collar work in ETO contexts.

To summarise, in this study, the ETO environment provides a new context that refines the theory on component commonality and its cost implications (for a more detailed discussion, see Lyly-Yrjänäinen 2008). Furthermore, this discussion is not only academically interesting but also provides some very interesting managerial implications.

MANAGERIAL IMPLICATIONS

The discussion in the previous section focused on the academically interesting results. However, the study provides interesting findings also for managers. Transaction drivers give the impression that, in terms of cost reduction potential, different components and component groups are just about equal. However, managers should be able to identify quite rapidly which group of components would most benefit from increased component commonality and, hence, would enable the most significant cost reductions. As a result, this study also introduces a strategy for identifying which group of components would most benefit from increased component commonality.

When a company starts to invest in increased component commonality, the development work might, at least initially, result in a slight cost increase, as shown on the left in Figure 4.3 (for a similar curve, see Labro 2003). However, when the commonality proceeds far enough, some cost

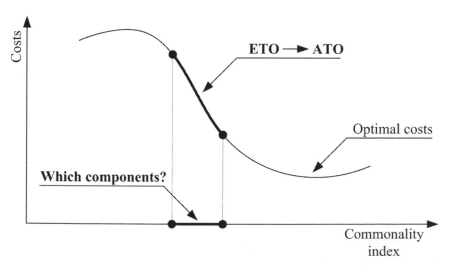

Figure 4.3   The components whose increased commonality enables the most significant cost reduction (curve modified from Labro 2003).

savings will be achieved (shown in the middle of Figure 4.3). In this study, the most significant process changes and thus also the most significant cost reductions are not achieved until the rethinking of the product architecture enables the ETO business to have at least some characteristics that are typical of an ATO business.

Instead of optimal costs (typical of published studies and shown on the right in Figure 4.3), managers were actually more interested in finding ways to reach the steepest part of the cost curve. In other words, managers wanted to identify those components in which the increased commonality would be likely to result in the most significant cost reduction because that would have provided the best return on investment. Managers simply were not that interested in cost optimisation, typically highlighted in the extant component commonality literature.

RESEARCH INTERVENTION

As discussed previously, the research focus shifted from wholesale operations to power unit manufacturing as the research collaboration advanced. Their previous experience in mass customisation motivated the managers of the case company to involve the researchers in the development of that business area. As seen in Figure 4.4, a hydraulic power unit includes large numbers of different commodity components (drives, pumps, valves, sensors etc.) assembled on top of a steel tank and steel frame. Because the user applications are often customer-specific, the hydraulic power unit also needs to be customised and engineered to order. ETO approach makes the

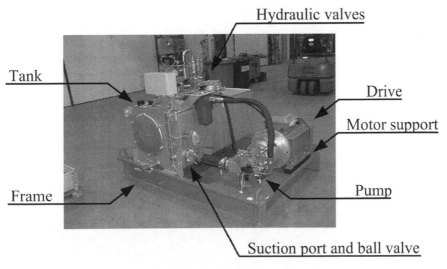

Figure 4.4   Example of a hydraulic power unit.

business very customer-oriented, but at the same time, it causes additional costs and lengthy delivery times. When the research collaboration started, the power unit business of the case company was barely breaking even and so the company was experiencing pressure to reduce costs.

According to the industry paradigm, power units were (and had to be) customised ETO products. Thus, in order to change the business, the researchers first had to demonstrate that the existing industry paradigm could be changed using the ideas of mass customisation. This was easier said than done—it eventually took several years and required a number of interventions both in product and process development. Furthermore, in order to study the possible cost implications, some management accounting practices needed to be improved as well. In order to illustrate the research process and the role of the researchers in it, the most important research interventions are shown in Figure 4.5.

The first year was primarily spent on becoming familiarised with the power units and their manufacturing processes. The main field researcher

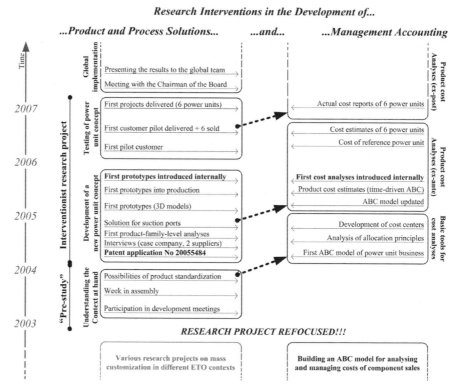

Figure 4.5   Research interventions into the case company.

was appointed as a member of the development team focusing on the development of the power unit business and, as a team member, the researcher started to participate in monthly development meetings. As a member of the team, the researcher also became involved in various assignments related to the development of the power units. At the beginning, most of these exercises were related to the modularisation of power units, a process that had already been started by the case company.

In the summer of 2003, the researcher spent a week in the assembly room to get first-hand experience of the product and its assembly process. Participation in the assembly work provided an excellent opportunity to learn about the technical aspects of the product and the product as a cost object. The informal discussions that took place with the employees during that week also helped to establish personal relationships with the assembly workers. During 2003, consideration was also given to whether some product standardisation would be possible. Many different exercises were carried out with the managers but without good results—the customers' specific requirements simply seemed to be too numerous to be fulfilled by a family of standardised power units.

In the spring of 2004, a new three-year research project was launched. As the first arrow in Figure 4.5 illustrates, initial participation in the product and process development had increased the researchers' understanding of power unit manufacturing and thus also provided a good starting point for development of costing practices in that business area. As a result, during the following year, an ABC model was built, the cost assignment principles of the company were analysed (and also updated) and some new cost centres were established in order to improve the traceability of costs. The main objective of this phase was to increase cost awareness among the managers and also to provide the tools needed for analysing cost implications of the new product solutions the managers were aiming at. In a sense, the costing systems were 'tuned up' to enable analyses of the potential cost implications of component commonality.

When the three-year research project was started, both the researchers and the managers were still effectively stumbling in the dark. However, in the summer of 2004, the development team finally began to achieve some progress. The hydraulic systems were configured using commodity components and so the customer-specific configurations could be handled with a set of interchangeable modules, as already attempted by the company. The problem, however, was that each customer-specific hydraulic system (i.e., a combination of components and modules) required the mechanical parts (tanks and frames in Figure 4.4) to include proper mounting surfaces. Thus, because the hydraulic system in each power unit was unique, these mechanical parts (especially the tanks) always needed some customisation.

The tank is the physical platform of the product and, as a result, it is needed first in the assembly. However, the tank cannot be designed until all the components of the power unit have been defined by the project engineers. Thus, the mechanical engineering of customised tanks was identified as the most important bottleneck for the delivery process. The tank can be seen as a low value-added part (it causes only 3–5 percent of the total cost), but because it represents a clear bottleneck, it always brought about many indirect costs, especially with respect to project-management-related activities. It was concluded that, to eliminate the need for customer-specific mechanical engineering of each tank, customised power units should be built with 'over-specified' common tanks. Similar to other studied ETO contexts (Lyly-Yrjänäinen 2008), this supported the idea of increased commonality of these low-value-added steel parts and, therefore, clearly focused the research interest on component commonality and its potential cost implications.

This was clearly a leap forward in the process of changing the industry paradigm, but it was not yet enough. Interestingly, in the autumn of 2003, the main field researcher had developed another patented solution for mass customisation of conveyor systems (Patent No. FI 117935) but it was not until the summer of 2004 that the researchers realised that the basic idea of that solution might also be applied to the power units (Patent application No. FI 20055484 in Figure 4.5). This realisation is what eventually fuelled up the development process. During that summer, some case company employees and suppliers were interviewed to test the feasibility of the solution in the hydraulic power unit business. According to those interviews, the solution seemed to solve most, though not all, of the technical problems related to customisation. The interface for attaching the pump to the tank (the so-called suction port shown in Figure 4.4) still needed some development.

In order to solve the problem related to the suction ports, the researchers analysed hundreds of different pump-drive module options and their impact on the tank. In a sense, the researchers were creating a product family of the theoretical product options that ETO customers might be ordering (first product-family-level analyses in Figure 4.5). The aim of this analysis was to understand the power units at the product family level, which was new to managers used to operating in the ETO context. ETO contexts do not have explicitly defined product families because products are designed only after customers have bought them. The rationale for the researchers' role in the above analysis was that the managers experienced in the ETO approach did not have the right mindset or competencies needed for such analyses—it was hard for them to question the industry paradigm. The project engineers did not even seem to understand why someone should study the bills of materials (BOMs) and tanks of power units not yet ordered by anyone. In other words, whereas the managers were used to defining the mounting surfaces of the tanks case by case, the researchers were attempting to analyse how different module options affect the tank in order to identify possible patterns that could facilitate the discovery of new solutions for mass customisation and, hence, increased component commonality of these tanks.

Despite the workload, this process eventually paid off and the analyses inspired a new idea for standardising the suction ports (solution for suction ports in Figure 4.5). Once this idea was born, the researchers learnt to use the company's three-dimensional computer-aided design (3D CAD) system and spent hundreds of hours making 3D models. Two important reasons have been identified as to why it was the cost management researchers that were doing this. First, the ETO approach is very burdensome for design resources and there simply was not enough engineering capacity available. Secondly, as discussed previously, the design engineers would not have had the knowledge to design such solutions because the product concept was so different from the ETO approach. Eventually, in the summer of 2005, the concept had evolved enough for the first prototypes to be manufactured (see Figure 4.5).

As shown in Figure 4.5 (the second arrow), the solution for the suction ports initiated another set of research interventions into cost management procedures. Because the costing practices had already been improved, there now existed good tools for *ex-ante* product cost analyses. To support these analyses, cost structures of numerous ETO power units were analysed in order to understand the cost structure of a power unit at a detailed level. The process of making *ex-ante* cost analyses also initiated very interesting discussions about the potential cost implications of increased component commonality. In those discussions, the concerns emphasised by the managers were the very issues that had also been highlighted in the existing component commonality literature (namely, the cost of over-specification and the use of transaction drivers). Managers were very concerned whether the additional holes needed for the over-specified common tanks would make them too expensive. In addition, they also wanted to have simple cost drivers that would be easy to measure reliably so that potential cost behaviour could be identified in an objective way.

However, the relevance of the extant theory on component commonality and its cost implications was quickly questioned. The team started to share the idea that over-specification resulting in additional holes would not increase component unit costs that significantly. The number of holes was not the problem but rather the complex information exchange needed in order to manufacture the project-specific holes. In addition, the team also started to share the opinion that tanks were developed in order to eliminate various project-management-related white-collar activities and not to reduce assembly times. Unfortunately, changes in the activities of project or sales engineers were difficult to quantify using simple transaction drivers. Batch size or the number of components simply did not seem to reflect the cost implications of process changes in these white-collar activities. As a result, the development team followed the basic idea of time-driven ABC and identified potential changes in the cost structure that were enabled by the mass-customised (common) tank. These *ex-ante* cost estimates started to clarify the cost reduction potential for all managers involved in the process, and enabled them to understand the main objectives of the development process. Instead of designing cheaper tanks, the objective was to design tanks that would reduce the amount of project engineering and sales engineering needed for customised power units. In the autumn of 2005, the first prototypes and related cost analyses (*ex-ante*) were introduced internally and the development work continued.

In the spring of 2006, the case company delivered a power unit to one important customer with large volume potential. At that point, costing practices had been improved by the researchers so *ex-post* cost analyses were considered fairly reliable. In addition, the delivered ETO power unit could have easily been replaced with a power unit using the mass-customised, common steel parts. Thus, the idea was born to use this ETO power unit as a reference point for analysing the costs of the first mass-customised power unit and, as a result, an *ex-ante* cost analysis was made for a functionally comparable mass-customised power unit. This was then compared with the *ex-post* cost analysis of the delivered ETO power unit.

The cost analysis was also shown to the customer, with highly positive feedback. In contrast to expectations, the customer requested only a few very minor technical changes. In fact the customer became so interested that it wanted one power unit that it had recently ordered but had not yet had delivered to be built using the new solutions. As a result, this customer became the first pilot customer (see Figure 4.5) and, typical in ETO contexts, there was now a project to which to assign the design resources needed for finalising the new product solution. The following day, the customer ordered an additional six power units, requesting that the new solutions should be used in them as well. Thus, in addition to the possibilities presented by using the project for piloting the new product solutions, these power units once delivered to them also provided *ex-post* cost data on the mass customised products. The cost analyses showed that the estimates done during the development process were fairly accurate and that the new solutions were indeed reducing the total costs. Without revealing the actual cost data, it can be concluded that, with the new solutions, the price level of power units came down about 10 percent without jeopardising the profitability level. At the same time, the delivery time was halved.

To summarise, much work had to be done with the managers in order to reach an *emic* level understanding of the phenomenon and, more importantly, the status of an expert in the field. This case also illustrates how the 'expert role' of the researcher can actually evolve during such long-term research collaboration. First, the researchers had some experience on similar mass customisation projects focusing on increased commonality in ETO contexts. That experience was from a different industry but with the ETO context as a common factor. Active participation in the development of products and business processes, combined with the work done on cost reporting practices, nevertheless helped the researchers to reach expert status in the industry at hand as well. But in order to reach that position, it was necessary for the researchers to do lots of practical development issues themselves; many things simply would have not evolved quickly enough, if at all, if the researchers had not been pushing things forward. This took the focus away from more theoretical research, but at the same time, it was crucial for the success of the project and, hence, indirectly also for the achievement of an interesting theoretical contribution.

This case was an example of how research interventions helped to gain the *emic* level access to the reality experienced by the practitioners and, hence, increase also theoretical understanding on component commonality and its cost implications. Interestingly, the key findings are relatively self-evident, nevertheless not discussed in the existing literature. However, it took quite some time of hands-on work in this new context to realize the importance of the context itself. In addition, the hands-on work focused mainly on non-accounting areas even though the major contribution of the research project still was to be in the area of management accounting. The next chapter focuses on a research project in which the role of non-accounting interventions in accounting research is emphasized.

5 Non-Accounting Interventions in Accounting

Chapter 4 showed a case where management accounting researchers were very intensively involved not only in development of accounting practices but in product development itself. In that chapter, the analysis concentrated on ways to gain insider, *emic* level access to the case company. This chapter will describe a case with some similarities, but this time our analysis will focus on the role of non-accounting interventions in management accounting research. This chapter discusses research extending over the period 2002–2008.

This chapter will show how the research collaboration has gradually evolved from costing into the area of service R&D and its management accounting implications. The nature of the research interventions is shown in Figure 5.1.

As seen in Figure 5.1, the research interventions are very strong, but at the same time, they are not so focused on management accounting. However, even though the research interventions were not directly related to

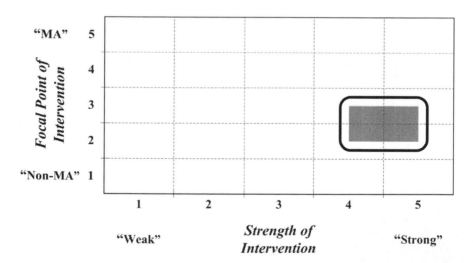

Figure 5.1 The interventionist role of the researchers in this research process.

management accounting, this chapter will show that they had clear connections with management accounting practices and also contributed to management accounting research.

MANAGEMENT ACCOUNTING RESEARCH WHEN SHIFTING FROM GOODS TO SERVICES

Vargo and Lusch (2004) describe a fundamental shift in the literature on marketing; in the new 'service logic', service provision rather than goods is fundamental to economic exchange. Moreover, customer relationships, intangibles and the co-creation of value with the customer form the basis of any service business. Meanwhile, the infusion of services into manufacturing is making a very timely appearance in the literature on services (cf. Oliva and Kallenberg 2003; Johansson and Olhager 2004). Several positive outcomes have been connected with this shift, including—to name but a few—extra invoicing, enhanced profitability, steadier cash flow and better corporate image (Mathieu 2001; Malleret 2005).

Although the service logic is said to be applicable in all business areas, manufacturing companies seem to have struggled quite considerably when taking their first steps towards being service providers. When looking at the transition of OEMs to being service providers, one must bear in mind that not all services are billable from the OEM's viewpoint. On the contrary, customers tend to regard many service offerings merely as 'good customer service' (e.g. Grönroos 2000; Malleret, 2005). Moreover, although manufacturers aim at becoming service providers, only a few of them have achieved the financial objectives associated with the service business (Gebauer et al. 2005). In many cases, expectations seem unrealistic, especially when compared with the actions taken.

In the business-to-business environment, decisions may require long processes involving many participants. Day and Herbig (1990) remind us that industrial goods often diffuse more slowly than consumer goods. However, the diffusion process may have more permanent consequences in the industrial sector. Thus, resources are needed to analyse what has actually changed or is currently changing in businesses when industrial companies are shifting their emphasis from physical products to different service solutions. More importantly, there are interesting management accounting related issues to be tackled. For example, how does the transition taking place in the manufacturing industry impact costing practices and cost management priorities?

RESEARCH OBJECTIVES AND RESEARCH SETTING

The basis for this research project is long-lasting co-operation between the case company's representatives and CMC. In the early 2000s, CMC had conducted research on projects aimed at the development of the company's supplier network (discussed further in Chapter 7). In terms of the research collaboration, the transition into after-sales business started in 2001 when a two-year research project focusing on warranty costs was started. Figure 5.2 illustrates the evolution of the research collaboration from the development of costing practices into services.

The project focusing on warranty costs showed the company's lack of knowledge regarding the cost and profit implications of after-sales services, laying the ground for a project focusing on the possibilities of moving forward in the value chain. A current status analysis of the company's service business (2003–2004) revealed that there was no consensus within the company on the nature of, and objectives connected with, the service business. This highlighted the need to explore the economic consequences of new service business, both within the company and among manufacturers more generally. After that analysis, the research focus was therefore more intensively placed on the development of service concepts for the case company. After that three-year research project ended in the summer of 2006, planning for yet another two-year project was started, and this was conducted in 2007–2008. This project continued the work already started in the previous project, and despite the gap in project funding, empirical work was done as if there had been an on-going five-year research project.

As the story above shows, the researchers got involved in the development of new service technologies step by step.

> Thus, the research collaboration with the company has aimed at understanding services as cost objects and, more generally, at the cost implications when manufacturing companies attempt to evolve into service providers.

It is noteworthy that the objectives of each project were identified during the on-going research agenda between the parties involved. In other words, the projects at hand consisted of a set of actions taken by the company and CMC representatives in order to fulfil the overall objectives of the long-lasting research co-operation.

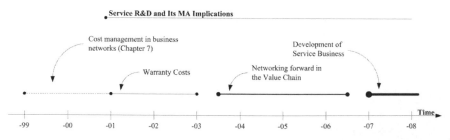

Figure 5.2   Evolution of the research collaboration as a series of research projects.

The longitudinal nature of the research co-operation enabled access to service R&D projects that are normally considered to be highly confidential in nature. The project manager of these research projects in the company, the R&D director, described the co-operation between CMC and the company as follows in 2005:

> *The basic research in the area of management accounting has already, for several years, been outsourced to CMC.*

It is noteworthy that one CMC researcher had access to the company and its databases during the project (2003–2008). The company representatives recognised that beneficial results from this kind of research project require a detailed level analysis of the particular phenomena at hand. Unless the researcher is given extensive access to the actual data and documentation of the company, the analysis inevitably remains superficial and is not likely to have significant practical contribution.

In order to illustrate the research setting, it is important to point out that Figure 5.2 mainly shows the funding structure of the research collaboration. In other words, Figure 5.2 only shows how the research collaboration has been organised in terms of project administration with the external research funders. The research collaboration with the company itself has continued quite seamlessly across these research projects. In terms of access to the company, the researchers were intensively involved in three service R&D projects carried out inside the company. In this chapter, references to these three projects mean the service R&D projects going on in the case company, as shown in Figure 5.3.

These three projects also show interesting elements in terms of research access. First, the project focusing on warranty costs (see Figure 5.2) demonstrated the need for the company to better understand its warranty costs and, more importantly, to manage them better. Thus, in a sense, the research project was a catalyst for establishment of a service R&D project focusing on extended warranty and its business opportunities (indicated by the arrow in Figure 5.3). Because the research collaboration was an

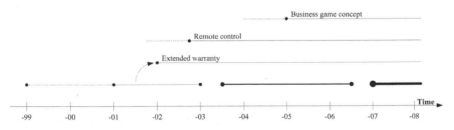

Figure 5.3   Service R&D projects going on in the case company used as empirical material for this study.

important catalyst for the project focusing on extended warranty, it was only natural for the researchers to be involved in the project.

Secondly, remote control technologies formed a project that had been going on in the company for some time, focusing mainly on the technological development needed for such services. To bring more of a business perspective on the development work, the researchers were also asked to join in that project. When looking at the role of the researchers, the findings from these first two projects are based mainly on occasional participation, interviews and analyses of existing reports and documentation, enabled by extensive access to the company's information systems. There were not interventionist elements in them which were that intensive—the researchers were acting rather as data gatherers and analysts. However, despite the lack of very deep interventions, access to the empirical data should not be undervalued—the researchers were allowed access to the company's ERP system to do analyses on their own. Such access is not at all common for external researchers.

The third project however, which focused mainly on the business game concept, was totally different. The case company had been developing a simulation tool that would help them to understand how their products behave under different conditions. The team involved in development of this simulation tool asked for the cost management researchers to help them implement some cost perspectives into the simulation model as well. Thus, an important aspect was to negotiate with the managers as to how the researchers could best facilitate that project. Interestingly, during those discussions, an idea about a business game surfaced. The company was developing the simulation model as a service that could generate revenue and so the business game was seen as an interesting way to make it more attractive for customers, especially if cost and profit perspectives were added into it.

In the project focusing on the business game, the CMC researchers acted as members of the R&D project team. The business game first focused mainly on selection of the right machinery for the right jobs. However, the researchers were able to integrate a financial and cost management module into the simulation game in a way that, in many cases, opened up the eyes of the players. Thus, the business game helped customers to understand how different investment decisions impact cost structure and profitability in their businesses. As the process went forward, the business game concept turned out to be a tool more suited to internal training than generating revenue by being sold to customer companies.

In this chapter, the research collaboration is briefly introduced in terms of motivation for the researchers' access to the company, the duration and nature of the interventions undertaken by the researchers during the project, and the practical and theoretical contribution gained from the project. Because the interventionist participation was deepest in development of the business game concept, the emphasis is put on that. However, some viewpoints from the other two projects are also given.

This case is also interesting because the company operates globally. Such multi-national companies usually have several stakeholders that, to different extents, either support or resist change, and power struggles and politics often delay the diffusion of new innovations. Nevertheless, the researchers were able to participate in developing service offerings in an international context involving other business units and organisations in other countries. Such participation has not been that common in management accounting research at all, let alone in interventionist management accounting research.

THEORETICAL CONTRIBUTION

During the first steps of the project, it became evident that some conceptual analysis focusing on the nature of service was needed in order to better understand the cost objects. As part of that analysis, it was proposed that 'service' means any activity done for the customer. In addition, different types of output of the activities, as well as different mechanisms of value creation, were identified. This study suggested that there do not seem to be generic characteristics of service that define service R&D projects as accounting objects. There are, however, context-specific characteristics that should be noted. The three service R&D projects analysed represent accounting objects that can be characterised as having a high relative degree of newness and significant uncertainty regarding the causes and effects of the key phenomena. These characteristics are significantly different from the R&D projects in machinery development that the company had been used to. Their typical R&D projects had strict and well-defined objectives and resource allocations, as well as only limited relative newness. Thus such service R&D projects represent new areas for companies that had heretofore been classified as machine providers.

Altogether, the project represents a learning process focusing on the characteristics of service, especially in a business context. Referring to the existing management accounting literature, it is unusual for real-life decision-making situations and accounting objects to be analysed in such a detailed manner and to be based on longitudinal data, such as in this study. In the accounting literature, based on the contingency theory, functional-level and project-level analyses have been requested instead of company or top management level analyses. Compared with more generic company level considerations, the sources and the multi-faceted roles of uncertainty as a contingency factor were identified and further examined. In particular, the role of the service phenomenon as a source of uncertainty was analysed more thoroughly than previously. The role of the identified contingencies was not analysed quantitatively, rather the focus was on the qualitative identification and description of those contingencies. There is a need for tools that enable a systematic analysis of projects and related products as accounting objects when they are already at an early stage in the R&D continuum. As an answer to this need, the approach employed in the project demonstrated its ability to provide a systematic approach to analysing projects with significant uncertainty involved.

Interestingly, the research project did not yield exact calculations regarding the economic consequences of the service R&D projects at hand, but focused more on exploration of the nature of those projects as accounting objects. In addition it is noteworthy that, on the basis of the longitudinal case study, it was possible to analyse the starting points, the actions taken and the results of particular service R&D projects in a detailed manner.

MANAGERIAL IMPLICATIONS

Following discussion with the managers, it was clear that the company expected tools/frameworks to estimate the economic potential of its new service business, and guidelines that would help it manage this type of R&D project, which had high levels of uncertainty. Although the machinery manufacturer was an experienced specialist in machinery R&D, projects where the machinery was actually in use by the customers represented a leap in the dark. Thus, even though explicit analytical tools were not developed, the project, nevertheless, significantly increased understanding of the financial and business implications associated with the transition from physical products to services. However, the main source of practical contribution from the research project was the business game concept developed with the help of CMC researchers.

Their deep involvement in the development of the business game concept and the introduction of financial elements into it provided very interesting results and initiated a process of internal development that is worth noting as one managerial implication of the research project. When the researchers became involved in development of the business game, the initial focus was on making the game a revenue-generating tool. In other words, the idea was to use the game to generate short term revenues from participants in the game events. However, as the project advanced and financial elements were also included in the game, the project team began to put emphasis on the internal learning process enabled by it.

Instead of using the game events as an additional service sold to customers, the game turned out to be a powerful tool for training the company's own staff to understand better how their customers think and evaluate different investment options. In other words, the key customer segment of the business game seemed to be the manufacturer's own personnel who would learn from the customers' production process and the role of their own machines in it. Even though the main output of the business game remained new information or knowledge, it still might be used as an input to the manufacturer's own processes, such as R&D or sales. However, in order to fulfil a variety of different information needs among the different functions of the manufacturer, the content and learning objective of the business game should be tailored for different participant groups in the future.

RESEARCH INTERVENTIONS

The interventionist role of the researchers varied depending on the service R&D project under investigation. As was pointed out previously, in the first two projects, the researchers were mainly data gatherers and analysts providing, nonetheless, interesting and valid information for decision-makers within the company. Only in the business game project did the interventionist role of the researchers become emphasised. Nevertheless, access in these other two projects to the company's empirical data was exceptionally good; only at the *emic* level was access to the decision-making processes not that deep.

In order to provide an overview of the research collaboration with the case company, Table 5.1 shows the steps of the overall research project. Six steps have been identified and, for each one, the methodology in use and the timeframe of each step are indicated. It is important to note that this research project represents an iterative learning process about the nature of service business for all parties involved, both researchers and practitioners. Remarkably, the steps C–F were not included in the initial project plan, but instead were initiated and clarified during execution of the project's first steps.

Table 5.1 The Key Steps of the Research Project

Step	Data, tools & methods	Time frame
Initialising	Interviews, meetings databases, reports	06–09/2003
Current status analysis of the service business	Interviews, cost analyses, meetings databases, reports	09/2003–11/2004
Literature review on service characteristics	Literature review, conceptual analysis, empirical illustrations	11/2003–12/2008
A business game concept	See detailed description	1/2005–10/2008
Analyses of the three service R&D projects	Longitudinal case study, participatory observations, interviews, databases, reports, documentation	11/2005–5/2008
Synthesis of the findings, reporting	Conceptual analysis, longitudinal case study	1–12/2008

Intervention by the researchers in the project may be classified as strong (see Figure 5.1) due to the longitudinal and intensive nature of the research co-operation with the case company management. When looking at the research collaboration in terms of numbers, altogether over 170 meetings were organised. In all these meetings, the researcher(s) and at least one participant of the case company were present. The duration of these meetings varied from one hour, small-scale meetings or interviews to more formal meetings with a number of people taking one or two days. The people present in these meetings represented several of the company's business units in twenty different countries. This gave the researchers access to the viewpoints of different factories and several front-line subsidiaries (i.e. sales offices). It is also noteworthy that, in addition to the 170 meetings just mentioned, up to fifteen representatives of seven different customer companies were met.

Due to its significance in the research project, the business game concept deserves closer attention. In the business game, a game event comprises three elements:

- Playing the game as teams
- Informative lectures focusing on business and production technology
- Discussions and reflections among the participants

The aim of the game is to gain a better understanding of customers' production processes. The teams make decisions about production (also production technologies and machine selections) and the economics of the customer company. They play several sessions during the game event in order to learn the causes and effects of their decisions. The concept is a competitive game, because competition motivates participation, and the game requires active participation during the event. The eagerness of the participants to win the game motivates them to seek for an optimal solution right up to the end of the game event. Thus, the desired learning outcomes from the game event include, first, an understanding of 'the big picture' of the customers' business and, secondly, recognition of the role of the company's machinery in its business.

The development process of the business game is shown in Table 5.2. The first stage (in the autumn of 2004) was to study the simulation model developed by the company. Despite the modest resources allocated to development of the simulation model, it covered a huge variety of different elements and had required profound knowledge of one production phase in customers' processes, which was provided by a team of specialists. However, for the simulation model to be used as an input in a business game, it required further development. Thus, in addition to the previously mentioned resources, the further development of this computer simulation model required some software developers to be hired for the project.

Table 5.2   The Key Steps of a Single Service R&D Project: A Business Game Concept

Step	Data, tools & methods	Time frame
Initialising	Meetings, analyses of the simulation tool	09–12/2004
Idea formulation	Project meetings, bench-marking	1/2005–4/2006
Concept development	Applied research: learning with games, game tools and environments, preliminary tests	4/2005–6/2006
Test games	Pilot customers, further development based on the feedback and observations of the experts	6/2006–7/2007
Preliminary use of the concept	Organising the game events, collecting feedback, refining the concept	8/2005–10/2008
Wrap-up	Documentation, identifying further possibilities	1–10/2008

Besides the simulation model of the customer processes, the business game required modelling of the availability, stand-by costs and usage costs of the machinery. This, evidently, was the responsibility of the researchers. In addition to the researchers, experts capable of making some lifetime estimates of different components also contributed to the project. As well as the internal resources, one pilot customer also participated in the development process. The managers of this customer company emphasised that the marketing management process related to the different end products would have to be included more fully in the game. According to this customer, the game should not only be about optimisation of its manufacturing processes and related financial impacts, but more realistically, it should also take into account the business realities the company faced. Moreover, the project team asked a pedagogue to assess the business game concept. Some issues of interest that arose from this assessment were, for example, how well the lectures, game sessions and related discussions enabled a cumulative learning process during the game event. As seen in Table 5.2, this idea formulation and concept development was an iterative process that took almost a year and a half, up to the summer of 2006.

Interestingly, decades ago, the initial development of the machinery had required knowledge in different areas, such as mechanics and hydraulics. In those days, specialists in the different fields had to be brought together to design state-of-the art machinery, whereas today the business units are self-sufficient in those areas. However, development of the business game concept forced the development team to cross business unit borders, seeking the best professionals in each area to give the various inputs needed for the business game. It was found that co-operation between the different business units (even in different countries) was relatively easy, because it was facilitated by an external party, the researchers.

During the following year, the business game was tested seven times with sixty people from different business units. This phase was the most active part of the project in terms of the resources employed and diffusion of the idea throughout the organisation. The company's personnel took care of the internal selling and planning of these test game events, while the researchers finalised the rules and tools of the game as well as the business lectures included in the game events. Some iteration was done based on the feedback from these test events but the content of the business game remained fairly constant during the project, so the project focused mainly on realisation of the initial idea. One major change, however, was that the duration of the game event evolved from a one-day game to a longer two-day 'tournament'.

Development of the business game concept represented an adventure in the customers' world, and the project team constantly learned new things related to the ways their customers think and the issues they really consider when purchasing equipment. These learning experiences—of the project team and, more importantly, of the company's personnel during the test game events—also resulted in a very interesting change regarding the objectives of the business game concept. As was previously pointed out, initially the emphasis was put on use of the business game among the customers as a means to generate service-based revenue. The internal test game events, however, revealed the huge potential this game had as a training tool for the company's own personnel. Thus the idea of process consultancy with steady cash flow was replaced by a model that emphasised the indirect benefits of the business game. The importance of such training tools should not be underestimated. Even if the business game itself is mainly used internally, external customers still benefit from it if the case company learns to particularise the needs of different customers and to develop and sell more suitable machinery and supportive services based on these specific needs. Nevertheless, this change in the main objective of the concept was not a self-evident issue; some managers of the company still wanted the business game to generate direct revenue.

At the moment, the future of the business game remains open. On the one hand, after the testing phase of the project the most important person in the project, the process specialist, was given another position inside the company—independent of the project. Consequently, for almost a year (6/2007–5/2008) the project was without a committed owner or active developer inside the company, a situation which can be nearly fatal to this type of project. On the other hand, dozens of company representatives had been made aware of the concept and the feedback had been very encouraging. With the new project owner taking responsibility for the project in June 2008, the game was played four times with forty more managers by the end of 2008, again with encouraging learning outcomes. The next steps regarding the business game remain, however, undecided by the company's top management.

It is noteworthy that the company and its customers had not actively thought of this type of product, which serves primarily as a learning facilitator. During a peak in machinery demand for the company and boom among its customers, development of this type of product is easily regarded merely as a secondary activity. Realisation of the recognised potential of the business game would require full-time resources to develop the game further and to diffuse it internally. The readiness of the HR function and other education resources in the company to disseminate the business game are currently being examined. Interestingly, the HR personnel are among the few company representatives who are already used to managing knowledge-intensive products.

With regard to the business game concept (and, to some extent, to the other two projects as well) the knowledge and expertise of the management accounting researchers were needed for the purpose of the R&D project itself. The idea behind the business game, for instance, came from several background phenomena in which the CMC representatives had earlier been involved. As noted, during a current status analysis of the service business the researchers found that, despite high expectations, the case company did not get much revenue outside pure machinery sales and traditional after-sales services (spare part sales). At this point, the R&D manager told the researchers that the company was keen to sell professional services. However, the company was not experienced in this area, and the customers regarded it as a traditional manufacturing company—more of a machine provider than a technology provider or partner in business development. The researchers advised that the intended change would require a new image which might be built by, for example, organising professional meetings among the key players in the industry and sharing some new process- and business-related knowledge with them.

In order to proceed with the search for new service products, the researchers analysed the key service technologies available in the company. In one meeting, a process specialist asked for advice on further development of the cost accounting part of their simulation model that focused on their customers' business. One idea had been to use the model as a means of supporting the consulting services. Consequently, the R&D manager, the process specialist and the researchers jointly developed the idea of the business game on the customers' business. The plan was for the business game concept to rely on the simulation model and the new cost accounting rules created by the researchers. At this point, the concept was seen as part of the planned professional meetings, to be used among the customers.

However, the idea of a business game did not come out of the blue. On the contrary, the researchers had for several years been intending to build a game to simulate and clarify the role of accurate (product) cost information in a rational decision-making process in companies. Thus, in a sense, the researchers had a personal interest in developing a sort of 'costing game' or 'management accounting game' while, at the same time, the case company had been thinking about something similar in order to evolve as a provider of knowledge-intensive services. Thus the idea of the business game was a sum of the various interests of the participants.

To conclude, the role of management accounting related interventions is very interesting because, obviously, the researchers were used as external experts in terms of cost modelling and cost analyses. However, in order to realise the business game concept most of the research interventions were not related to management accounting. Thus, the researchers were key drivers in terms of making the business game become a reality and, as a result, their efforts were needed in a wide range of areas. Involvement in such a process nevertheless gave very good access for gathering data on and understanding of services as cost objects, and how traditional OEMs can benefit economically from these value added services.

This case was on example of how the research interventions have gradually been moving away from management accounting itself more towards various tasks needed to understand the accounting context. Compared to the previous case, this time the involvement in the organization was not that holistic; researchers were not so deeply involved in the decision-making and, hence, this project was positioned in the Level 4.5. This project was used to illustrate how interventionist management accounting research provides interesting options to shed light on various contexts and, in that way, increase understanding on the role of management accounting in such contexts. Similarly, there are many other black boxes in the area of management accounting thus far overlooked by management accounting researchers. The next chapter will discuss a research stream where interventions were used for opening up such black boxes.

6 Opening the 'Black Boxes' in Accounting

One typical area in which CMC has been involved with numerous companies is how to provide product cost information for different decision-making situations. This chapter focuses on just one such case company, which has been involved in three different interventionist costing projects with CMC over the time period of eight years.

As has been pointed out by Jönsson and Lukka (2007), there are plenty of black boxes within MA practices in organisations that are worth looking into. This chapter focuses on using interventionist research in opening some of the black boxes in the area of management accounting. As seen in Figure 6.1, research interventions are relatively strong (almost a family). In addition, of all the six cases the interventions discussed in this chapter focus most clearly on development of management accounting practices.

Product costing is no longer assumed to have theoretically interesting research potential—it is, in the end, relatively simple—but there are still plenty of problems to solve in order for practitioners to access the product

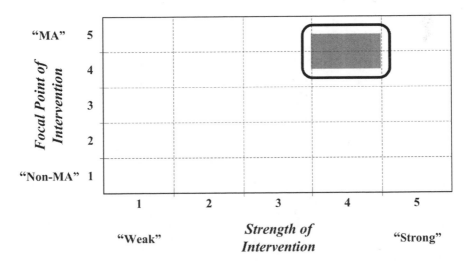

Figure 6.1 Research interventions in this case focus most clearly on the MA domain.

cost information they need. However, a good question is whether it is the role of researchers to solve those practical problems or not. When peeking inside the 'black box' of product costing or product profitability in different organisations, do there still remain interesting areas also in terms of management accounting research?

PRODUCT COST INFORMATION FOR DECISION MAKING

Information on product costs and product profitability is a pre-requisite for cost-conscious management. Only once cost information becomes available can the management make decisions that take into account the cost perspective. Cost information can be used for making decisions concerning product variety, product volumes, or marketing efforts (Sievänen et al. 2003). The so-called whale curve or Kanthal curve is the classical example, showing that only part of a company's products are profitable; a significant proportion only break even while some are unprofitable, eating up a significant part of the potential profits (see, for example, Kaplan and Atkinson 1998). Typically, both the most profitable and the least profitable products are among the best performers in terms of sales volume. In addition, such a whale curve is expected when ABC systems are implemented in a company in which indirect and support resources are high and there exists great diversity among products, customers and processes (Kaplan and Atkinson 1998). However, based on this case, the whale curve seems to apply also in contexts with low amounts of indirect costs and relatively homogeneous product assortment.

When attempting to improve product profitability, the impact of product development is crucial (Turney 1991; Uusi-Rauva and Paranko 1998). The importance of cost management during product development is highlighted by the perception that the scope for cost management once a product is launched is determined in large part by how it is designed (Asiedu and Gu 1998; Raffish 1991; Reinertsen 1997). However, in many businesses, after-sales service is a key issue affecting the total profitability of a product (Knecht et al. 1993; Wise and Baumgartner 1999). Accordingly, a company's product strategy should not be limited to supporting just new product sales if after-sales services have an essential impact on the company's profit (Johansson and Olhager 2004; Wise and Baumgartner 1999). Yet the financial management of product support activities is a relatively neglected area, both in the literature and practice; life cycle cost awareness within different organisations has generally been rather weak (Jackson and Ostrom 1980; Järvinen et al. 2004; Lukka and Granlund 1996). Thus, the previously mentioned whale curve has to be supplemented with information on life cycle profitability (that is profitability taking after-sales activities into account), which is another area tackled in this case.

Analysis of long-term profitability from the supplier's perspective reminds us that the notion of life cycle costing is more multi-faceted than is typically perceived (Woodward 1997). Life cycle costing does not have to be only about calculating and comparing investment costs with the costs of maintenance and use of a product (product-ownership-centric); it can also be more supplier-oriented, looking at the patterns that create profitable business with different kinds of products. After-sales has been perceived both as a key issue affecting the total profitability of a product and as generally very profitable business (Knecht et al. 1993; Wise and Baumgartner 1999). The after-sales profitability differences presented here (although deriving from a single case) point out the need to conduct more detailed investigations that seek out the causes and effects of after-sales profitability.

RESEARCH OBJECTIVES AND RESEARCH SETTING

The case company is a globally operating organisation that develops, manufactures and assembles capital goods for industrial customers with an annual production volume of approximately 3,000 end products (at the time of this study). In the early years of the twenty-first century, the net sales and production volume of the company was increasing with a gross margin varying typically between 10 and 20 percent of net sales. At the time of this study, the net sales of the company totalled about 36 million Euros. Approximately 7 million Euros (about 20 percent) of total sales were derived from after-sales activities. Overall, the company had been profitable during recent years but—unfortunately—it did not know exactly which of its products were profitable.

The range of products supplied by the case company includes nearly 100 different customisable products, leading to hundreds of possible product variants. The manufacturing process of these products consists mainly of assembly work. However, in addition to assembled products, the company also manufactures the main components for these products. At the time of the study, 25 different models of the main component were in production. Of these models, some were sold to other manufacturers, and some models were manufactured only for the company's own assembly. Despite the large number of different products, the product range of the company was still relatively homogenous, size being the main difference among models. In other words, the production processes of different products were quite similar, with differences mainly existing in work cycle times and batch sizes.

The typical cost structure of an assembled product is dominated by direct material costs, which usually represent about 70 percent of the total cost. The costs associated with direct manufacturing activities correspond to 20 percent of total cost and the amount of indirect costs to about 10 percent of total cost. Compared with assembled products, the share of material costs for main components decreases to approximately 50 percent of the total whereas direct manufacturing costs cover about 40 percent and indirect activities about 10 percent. It was generally assumed that main component production was more profitable than assembled product production. On the other hand after-sales business, which was mainly connected with assembled products, was assumed to be very profitable, thus compensating for the relatively low profitability of end-product sales. By and large, however, these perceptions were nothing but speculation because there were errors in the bills of material, problems in assigning indirect costs to products or components and, especially, problems in assigning after-sales profits to corresponding products.

The lack of product level cost and profitability information was the main reason for the company to engage in an interventionist research project with CMC. In this setting, CMC was interpreted as an expert organisation in the field of product costing, and the company decided to utilise external resources for improving its product-level cost-consciousness.

> *Thus the projects conducted in collaboration with the company were focusing rather generally on increasing cost awareness within the company, which later on opened up interesting streams for management accounting research.*

The start of the project was partly the result of a coincidence, as the managing director of the company had encountered a representative of CMC at a meeting and heard a presentation about CMC. This led to a series of discussions between the company and CMC, during which the motivation to work together was identified. Without revealing all the details of this process, in summary access was based on three things:

- The company's need to acquire more reliable and detailed product level cost information for profitability management
- CMC's reputation and knowledge-base in the field
- Available external (public) funding that partly facilitated the establishment of the formal research project.

Collaboration with the company was organised as a series of distinct research projects, each one with some external public funding in them. These three research projects are shown in Figure 6.2. However, in this chapter, the main emphasis is on the two first projects, focusing on product profitability and the impact of after-sales business on product profitability. The dashed line in Figure 6.2 means that there still was some collaboration with the case company during 2003 and 2004, yet without either a formal research project or significant project funding.

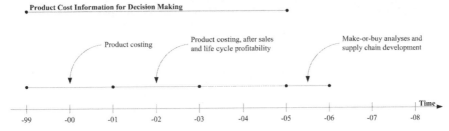

Figure 6.2 The long-term research collaboration has been organised in three research projects.

From the company's perspective, therefore, the project was initially mainly seen as a development project focusing on cost information improvement. For CMC, the project was not primarily seen as a vehicle for producing specific theoretical contribution but rather it represented a natural setting for learning more about the role of cost information in manufacturing. In that sense, the starting point was very much an open-ended exploration of real-life and, thus, interesting research questions were not identified by the researchers prior to the project's commencement. However, despite this, CMC's collaboration with this company and intensive, hands-on participation in the development of costing practices has still provided empirical material for academically interesting research.

THEORETICAL CONTRIBUTION

As was pointed out previously, the whale curve is expected when ABC systems are implemented in a company where indirect and support resources are high and there exists great diversity among products, customers and processes (Kaplan and Atkinson 1998). However, in the case company, the processes needed for manufacturing the main components for different end products and also for the final assembly are quite homogeneous. The main differences are found in cycle times, because larger products simply need more time. In addition, indirect costs only account for about 10 percent of the total costs. In this sense, the case company does not quite fulfil the criteria typically present in a heterogeneous product-level profitability situation. Nevertheless, it was found that the cumulative product profitability follows an archetypal whale curve, with the peak (only) at 177 percent. Most of the products had only a modest effect on the total profitability, primarily due to low production volumes. At the same time, the most unprofitable 20 percent of products contributed 55 percent of the reduction in the company's total profit.

The cost structures of profitable and unprofitable products were analysed further without finding any significant difference. It was instead argued that profitability was strongly related to the products' competitive situation within their market. The most profitable products were those that could offer the best savings for customers in terms of their operation expenses. The most unprofitable products were those that attempted to enter a market with seemingly tight price competition. Furthermore, products in the decline phase of their life cycle were the most unprofitable.

Even though some of the products were found to be unprofitable, when taking into account a long-term perspective there were different profitability profiles between products. It was stated previously that the scope for cost management once a product is launched is determined in large part by how it is designed (Asiedu and Gu 1998; Raffish 1991; Reinertsen 1997). While this is mainly true from the cost perspective, the situation is somewhat different from the profitability perspective. Customer profitability and long-term product profitability can be greatly influenced by decisions during the after-sales period. Figure 6.3 shows the impact of after-sales on product profitability at the unit level. It shows that some products which are unprofitable from the new-product sales perspective are, in fact, profitable when the after-sales perspective is taken into account. However, with some products, the after-sales perspective cannot be used as a justification for selling the products at an unprofitable price.

As a whole, the results emphasise the limitations of an approach to product profitability assessment that is too narrow, and also the need to take a longer, life cycle view of both primary and ancillary product sales. More generally, the results show that the problems identified in the literature regarding life cycle considerations can be partly overcome by utilising existing costing techniques—not perhaps continuously but at least on an occasional basis.

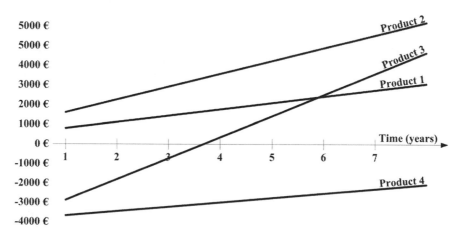

Figure 6.3   Life cycle profitability of end products as a function of time, considering both new product and after-sales activity.

MANAGERIAL IMPLICATIONS

Overall, these interventionist research projects resulted in an increase in the level of cost-consciousness among the company representatives. The assumptions regarding product costs and product profitability were replaced with knowledge based on cost analyses. This was remarked on by a number of people at different levels in the case company.

In addition to costs, pricing behaviour was also analysed as part of the study. Price is obviously the other component in product profitability but it is not often discussed profoundly in cost management literature. However, in real life, pricing is another area where many assumptions are made by managers. It was very interesting to see how management thinking evolved in terms of pricing.

RESEARCH INTERVENTIONS

As was pointed out previously, the research collaboration with the case company was organised in three different research projects. The first project was solely focused on the development of costing practices and the major outcome was a costing model using the principles of ABC. Two researchers were involved in this development process which, naturally, was done in close collaboration with the case company managers. Management participation was needed in order to gather various input data to be used in the costing model though it was not intended for operative use but rather for supporting the *ad hoc* analysis of product costs and profitability.

In terms of the research interventions, researchers were considered as experts in product costing. There were many issues that they needed to analyse and define when building the actual cost model, such as the level of detail the model should be taken to, cost objects, activities, processes and resource groups. Obviously, the researchers did not know the answers on all these issues and so one important impact was to make the managers and employees think about their work and how to handle it in the costing model. In other words, the managers and employees were made to analyse their own work and the different cause-and-effect relationships while the researchers then transferred this information into inputs for the cost model.

The costing model was eventually used to identify product-level profitability of all the case company's end products, represented as a whale curve. This information was then shared among the managers, initiating a series of interesting discussions on various factors that explained the differences in profitability. In a sense, the cost analysis was merely a starting point for more interesting research work. After these results were shown to the managers, many other analyses were made in order to find the reasons behind the good or bad profitability of different products. Because of the large amount of work invested in building the costing model, it was possible to do more detailed analyses explaining some of the differences than would otherwise have been the case (for a more detailed discussion, see Sievänen et al. 2003). Thus without the strong interventions in the early stages of the research collaboration, there would not have been any basis for more interesting interventions that, in the end, also resulted in major theoretical contributions.

The second project continued with the interventions in management accounting and, based on a request by the company, an attempt was made to develop a costing model that would better respond to the flexibility of and rate of change in the business. Thus the costing model that had been built in the first project was iterated in order to respond to the changes. Interestingly after this second version of the costing model was finished, the company's representatives raised a number of questions on the basis of the cost and profitability information it produced that then led to closer attention to after-sales profitability:

> *What about the profitability of the after-sales connected to these products?*

In terms of tracking down the impact of after-sales on product profitability, it was necessary to understand more about the spare part and service sales for different product models. This was analysed using the existing maintenance plans of different product models, which naturally assumed that spare parts are bought from the company and pirate parts are not used. As was shown in Figure 6.3, not all the unprofitable products reached break-even point even when the potential revenues of after-sales were taken into account. Thus after-sales, which is generally perceived as very profitable, is a fertile ground for detailed financial analysis. For example, the contribution made by after-sales to product profitability is strong but differs significantly between product groups.

As part of the project, life cycle profitability was evaluated by combining new product profitability and after-sales profitability. Through this it was possible to identify four categories of product with each one representing a different long-term profitability profile and requiring different actions. First, there were those products that are profitable both in terms of new product and related after-sales. In the case company this group was quite small, though it had substantial economic impact. Secondly there were products that were unprofitable both in terms of new product sales and after-sales. Naturally, these products were potential targets for re-design or abandonment though some of them were at the beginning of their life cycle and had not reached either a sufficient sales volume or population in the field. Between these two rather clear-cut categories there were two groups of products, the position of which is not self-evident. There were products whose overall profitability relied on a strong after-sales phase, in respect of which it is very important for the producer to achieve sufficient market share from the after-sales business. These products were identified as good targets for re-engineering. Finally, there were some products with unprofitable after-sales, for example because of pirate spare part suppliers. Despite the simplicity of the analysis described above, it increased awareness within the company that life cycle product and customer profitability analyses can enable it to capture a much greater share of each customer's business.

Another interesting area that was brought up as part of the process of building the iterated cost model was variation in the sales prices. This surfaced almost accidentally. Even though pricing is a key component in profitability management, it is not that often monitored systematically, which was the situation in the case company as well. It was assumed first by the researchers (and also by the managers) that price information needed for product-level profitability analyses could be derived from price lists and product catalogues. Thus, managers would have been very happy with profitability analyses based on average prices. However, at about the same time, the field researcher had a conversation with a sales engineer who promised to provide a database that had all the actual sales prices at the transaction level, which was then analysed systematically by the researcher. The analysis showed surprisingly large variations in actual prices. The sales people, however, did not consider that so relevant issue:

> OK, *there is some variation in the prices. However, the lowest and highest prices are nothing but some special cases, nothing to be paid attention to* . . .

This, obviously, raised the interest of the researchers and, as a result, the pricing was analysed in more detail, including all the end products and spare part items. The analysis showed that, in fact, there was a significant amount of variation in the pricing. It would be easy to say that volume is the key driver in pricing decisions, and this is what sales managers and sales people pointed out. However volume was not the factor that consistently explained pricing decisions in this case. Furthermore, the analysis did not include products that had been sold using transfer pricing within the group, which also took away some of the other explanations from the sales people.

Under such circumstances, a systematic monitoring of actual sales prices would be a powerful tool in profitability management. It is true that markets define the price level (the most typical argument of sales people), but at the same time, it is the responsibility of sales people to understand the implications of their pricing decisions. This analysis took quite some time but resulted finally in very interesting ways of analysing pricing. In addition, it also convinced managers and sales people about the true variability in product pricing. This was almost immediately an issue that was rather sensitive for the managers—they would not wish their customers to have access to such knowledge.

Once the research collaboration had advanced, the managers started to ask more and more questions and reveal information that they would not share with an outsider. One such area was variance in company-level profitability in monthly reports. It was bothering the parent company that the profitability of the case company tended to change rather dramatically from one month to the other. This had resulted in situations where people in the financial department had to try to come up with explanations for the parent company even though they had not been able to identify good reasons that explained the monthly variation. The analyses showed that there was surprisingly large variance in the sales prices and this was considered as one explanation for the variance in company profitability too:

> *The selling prices may vary, and explain a part of the variance on profitability.*

As a result, the researchers started to look at possible problems in the company's financial reporting practices, a task requested by the managers but not theoretically that interesting. The researchers analysed, for example, work-in-process inventory, allocation of salaries and wages, and possible problems in bills of materials (BOMs) that might distort material use, in order to eliminate at least some parts of the profit variation caused by problems in the reporting practices.

Variability in pricing practices was already a relatively sensitive issue but the variability in the monthly profits was definitely an issue the financial managers would not have wished to talk about with outsiders. Thus the increased trust among the participants was an important issue that enabled the researchers' access to interesting problems and discussions—but such a relationship takes years to evolve. In addition to the increased trust, the initial intervention—and especially its successful completion—resulted in additional questions that were also interesting from the point of view of theoretical contribution. In other words, even though there were no explicit research questions in mind when the research collaboration was started, the first results achieved opened up issues with interesting contribution potential.

The third project is, again, an example of the importance of long-term collaboration in interventionist research. When good results are achieved, especially in terms of pragmatic relevance, companies are willing to continue work with the researchers. However, because there had already been a lot of work done in the development of costing practices inside the organisation, this time the focus of development efforts could be wider, on supply chain development on the basis of cost data. The researchers were involved in the modelling of operations taking place between a key supplier and the case company. This development work resulted in open book discussions between the supplier and the case company and, in a similar way to the case discussed in the next chapter, the researchers participated as neutral, third-party facilitators in the open book negotiations between the two parties.

In summary, the majority of the interventions done during the series of projects were directly focused on management accounting in general and product costing in particular. In all three projects, the role of researchers was:

- To collect quantitative and qualitative data that can be utilised in product costing (cost and activity drivers, appropriate assignment and matching principles)
- To construct the cost model using relevant tools and systems
- To initiate discussions and learning on the basis of data
- To keep the momentum up—that is, to facilitate and co-ordinate the process of development of cost-consciousness

As we see it, the whole process could be seen very much as an iterative one, with each new round peeling a layer from something that was previously considered as a black box. For instance, only after a detailed elaboration of product level profitability did it became clear that the impact of after-sales on total profitability was substantial. This understanding was followed by a detailed investigation into the nature of after-sales profitability, which revealed that the profitability of after-sales was, in fact, very heterogeneous by its nature, which was not at all expected.

In terms of interventionist research, this project shows one very interesting element. Opening up these black boxes will most likely provide interesting and very useful information for the managers. However, opening them up is a big investment and, in terms of theoretical contribution, it may include significant risks, yet it is very difficult (if not impossible) to really justify beforehand what the contribution of the potential findings may be. In this case, the risk-taking paid off and some very interesting results were achieved. On the other hand, research has many similarities to other innovation contexts and, as a rule of thumb, one must work hard on different ideas and innovations to find the really successful ones.

This analogy to innovation processes and the related uncertainties is very interesting when looking at the mainstream management accounting research where the theoretical contribution should, preferably, be known already before starting the research project in the first place. This seems to be the case especially when attempting to make theory refinements by opening up black boxes such as in this case. Studying new and emerging topics, on the other hand, provides research settings where contribution potential is easy to argue even before the first visit to the well-selected case company. However, when studying new phenomena, the challenge is to, first, find organisations that already have implemented such novel management accounting tools or concepts and, second, to gain access to at least one of them. Interestingly, interventionist research provides one alternative way to solve this problem.

7 Studying New and Emerging Topics

For some management accounting innovations, it may take a long time before they are widely diffused in practice. Thus, it may be difficult to find and gain access to the first-mover organizations to study new management accounting innovations being implemented in the early stages of their life cycle. Interventionist research, however, may serve as a vehicle for catalysing such innovation processes in organizations where the researchers already have access or have easier access, hence facilitating the access to interesting empirical data.

This chapter discusses two research projects focused on cost management in business networks and, more specifically, on different facets of open book accounting. In fact, the first of the two research projects discussed here, together with another project discussed in the previous chapter, resulted in the establishment of CMC. Furthermore, the collaboration with the company discussed in Chapter 4 was started as a part of this very same project—it was one of the suppliers of the main contractor of the first inter-organizational cost management project discussed in this chapter. This well illustrates the interconnectedness of the research streams discussed in this book and also the continuous nature of the research collaboration. This chapter discusses research work done in inter-organisational cost management between 1998 and 2005, though the topic has actually been touched on in various other later projects as well, such as the one discussed in the previous chapter.

This chapter illustrates how research interventions can aim at creating a setting in which to study new and emerging topics. Thus, interventions can be seen as a substitute for (1) trying to find an environment where a certain chain of events is unfolding and (2) trying to get access to that process of events. The interventions discussed in this chapter are classified in Figure 7.1.

As seen in Figure 7.1, the research interventions discussed in this chapter mainly focus on management accounting though partly on other areas too, primarily inter-organisational collaboration. In addition, researchers have active and versatile participation and can be seen as 'almost family'.

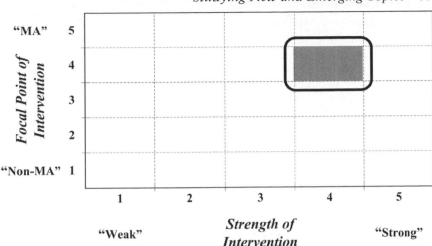

Figure 7.1 Focus and intensity of research interventions.

BACKGROUND—EXPLORING THE FACETS
OF OPEN BOOK ACCOUNTING

Inter-organisational cost management (IOCM) in general, and open book accounting (OBA) in particular, have been seen as a response by management accounting to the evolution taking place in many supply chains (Thrane 2007; Mouritsen et al. 2001; Cooper and Slagmulder 2004). In spite of the increased research activity in the field, however, detailed evidence on the application of these tools in real-life settings is still relatively sparse (see, for example, Kajüter and Kulmala 2005; McIvor 2001; Carr and Ng 1995) so in-depth case studies are sought to elaborate the interaction between companies engaged in various IOCM practices (Håkansson and Lind 2004).

Such studies are useful for several reasons. First increased outsourcing, the focus on core competences and low cost sourcing—just to name a few recent trends for supply chain development—extend the domain of cost management over the boundaries of a single business (Otley 1994). Broad discussion on IOCM and OBA, despite its merits, therefore needs to be complemented with detailed investigations into processes, procedures, techniques and applications of these in real-life settings. Otherwise, many details, such as those that shape the diffusion of OBA as an approach, may be left unveiled. Secondly, inter-organisational configurations can be so versatile that the roles and processes of cost management are likely to vary substantially from one instance to another (see van der Meer-Kooistra and Vosselman 2006). Without more empirical work, little is known about these likely variations within IOCM processes and their contextual connections, or about their contingent nature (Chapman 1997). Thus, more evidence is useful for understanding, and eventually developing, cost management practices that are well-aligned with specific development objectives and inter-organisational configurations. More elaborated theory on whether and how the techniques and procedures of OBA should be adapted to fit a given context are also pragmatically relevant. Finally, the association between open books and businesses' overall management control structure is more closely investigated in order to better understand the role of OBA in control packages (see Malmi and Brown 2008).

RESEARCH SETTING

The discussion in this chapter is based on two research projects aimed at development of IOCM practices in supply networks. The first project was conducted with Drill Inc., an original equipment manufacturer (OEM) company engaged in manufacturing mining equipment, and its eight strategic suppliers. The second project involved Excavator Inc., an OEM manufacturing excavators, and its five selected suppliers. However, the focus is on two cases where detailed product cost information was exchanged between the suppliers and the OEMs. These two cases present OBA as an accounting template (or strategy as phrased by Mouritsen et al. 2001) with a seemingly flexible character and, in this way, continue along the path mapped by Thrane and Hald (2006) by looking at the interplay between an accounting template (in this case OBA) and the context in which it is put to work.

> *The objective of the case studies discussed in this chapter is to shed light on the details of OBA process and the ways OBA can be applied in practice.*

The main interest in this long-term case study lies in the potentially versatile roles and meanings that might be associated with OBA in different organisational supply chain configurations. The companies involved in the empirical study are shown in Figure 7.2. As seen in this figure, some of the companies can be classified as system suppliers, some as parts manufacturers and, in the case of Drill Inc., some can be termed component suppliers (technical wholesalers providing various commodity components, like the one discussed in Chapter 4). Cost management practices were developed in six supplier companies and four of them chose to open their books to their OEMs. The arrows in Figure 7.2 show the customer-supplier relationships discussed in this chapter.

With both OEMs, the interventionist projects were preceded by several years of research collaboration (see Figure 7.3). Because of this mutual history, the researchers and managers in both OEMs alike were familiar

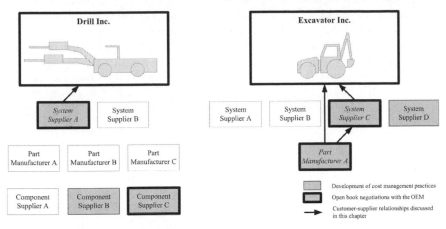

Figure 7.2   Companies involved in the two research projects and supply relationships discussed in this chapter.

with each other and the nature of interventionist research. Although the researchers' role in both networks was focused on the development of cost management practices, the managers had identified a number of wider objectives. The projects were expected to produce new processes and capabilities which would help participating companies to identify cost and profitability improvement possibilities, to seek ways to achieve improvements, and to support the allocation of realised benefits.

Joint cost management in a network requires that each company in the network is aware of its own costs (cf. Agndal and Nilsson 2009). Only after that is it possible to share cost information more widely and to try to find solutions to the observed problems collaboratively. During the fieldwork, researchers acted as change facilitators and participated in the process of creating more accurate and detailed cost information in participating companies. Given the relatively poor and heterogeneous status of cost information within the businesses, the information created was a precondition for the OBA process to start.

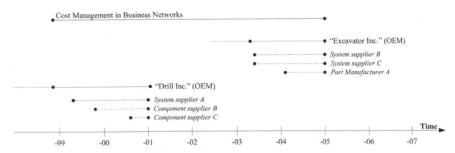

Figure 7.3   Timeline of the research project.

Because undeveloped cost management practices and the lack of accurate cost information are recognised as obstacles to OBA in general (see for example Kajuter and Kulmala 2005), research interventions aiming at improved cost information among the firms is an important justification for the selected research approach. Thus, the responsibility of the researchers was to increase cost awareness in order to enable inter-organisational cost management. The idea was that the development of cost management practices (and cost reporting in particular) with the suppliers would point out interesting targets for future development which could then be tackled across the entire network. In both projects, managers of the participating companies got together a few times a year for 'network gatherings' where the results were discussed and further actions decided together.

In both projects, research collaboration was started by analysing the cost management and cost reporting practices of the suppliers. This interview study formed the basis for selecting suppliers for more intensive development of cost management practices (shown in grey in Figure 7.2). For all selected suppliers, activity-based cost (ABC) models were built, focusing on components delivered to the OEMs. The researchers were the ones responsible for developing the ABC models, though in collaboration with the managers. This meant that the researchers had excellent access to the management practices of all the selected suppliers.

Once costing practices had been improved within the selected suppliers, the OEMs obviously were interested in gaining access to the resulting cost information. Out of the six selected suppliers, four agreed to open their books to the OEM (illustrated with thick lines in Figure 7.2). During the process, researchers were responsible for arranging and chairing the meetings where the cost information related to parts and components delivered to the OEMs was revealed. Thus, in addition to cost information providers, researchers acted as neutral partners and facilitators in OBA negotiations between companies.

Although cost management practices were developed in six companies and four of them actually opened their books for their main contractors (OEMs), this chapter will not describe all the events that took place. Instead, we focus on two of the OBA processes and the events that took place in them. The customer-supplier relationships involved in the OBA processes are shown by the arrows in Figure 7.2. The first case involves Drill Inc. and its system supplier, while the second case involves Excavator Inc. plus one system and one component supplier. These two cases have been selected because they illustrate contrasting results and thus represent theoretical replication (Yin 1994) within OBA. The first case provides a partnership view in which collaboration played an important role. In the second case, two selected suppliers were made to compete with each other and the cost information provided by the neutral third party was used to force the existing supplier to take the actions requested by the OEM.

Even though these two selected cases represent contrasting interpretations of OBA, the research settings do not differ too much from each other. In both cases, the products are rather similar (machinery) and even the industries and the practices within these industries are alike. Despite the fact that the second case took place a few years later than the first, both cases were conducted under favourable economic cycles. Furthermore, both industries can be seen as fairly mature and they both are in need of continuous cost reduction. Thus, suppliers can no longer expect to raise their price annually; on the contrary, they have to agree to take initiatives to find ways to reduce prices constantly. Finally, in both cases, the same two researchers were responsible for the projects.

RESULTS AND THEORETICAL CONTRIBUTION

This case presents OBA as an accounting template with a seemingly flexible character and provides theoretical contribution in four areas. First, it is useful to see the practice of OBA as a process (a series of activities) and understand the flexibility that derives essentially from the goal-setting of that process. Thus, goals that are attributed to open books have a great impact on the nature of the OBA exercise. So far, the current literature has not sufficiently opened the 'black box' of OBA (see Thrane et al. 2008).

Secondly, and as a consequence of observed flexibility, it is stressed that open books should not be connected exclusively with partnering (cf. Mouritsen et al. 2001) but should be seen more openly as a possible part of even quite opposite control strategies (Speklé 2001). Thirdly, and to be more specific, in the partnering context open books have proved their capability as a component of exploratory control (for example, Cooper and Slagmulder 2004; Dekker 2003) but they might also play a role in situations characterised by market control or even boundary control. However, this does not imply that open books are necessarily a best fit with those settings.

Finally, open books may serve as a vehicle for affecting the control determinants, especially by improving the programmability of performance. To our knowledge, this has not been identified in the extant literature either.

MANAGERIAL IMPLICATIONS AND
PRACTICAL CONTRIBUTION

When looking at the managerial implications of the research projects, in the first case it seems that the open book negotiations helped to create a positive relationship between the OEM and the system supplier. Demonstrating this, after the first open book negotiations cost analysis was expanded to include all the products that the supplier was delivering to the

OEM. Furthermore, the exercise served to set the standards for how the OEM wanted to work with its strategic suppliers. Even several years after the actual research project, the senior managers of the OEM still point out the results achieved in that project.

You should consider it as a point of reference.

This first case is a very interesting one in the sense that the research interventions have provided results that have survived even though the researchers have already made their exit—it is often a major risk that the results achieved in the research project survive only as long as the researchers/facilitators remain in close connection with the organisation. The first case also raised lots of managerial interest in Finland and the main results were published as a managerial business book (Seppänen et al. 2002, in Finnish).

In addition, despite the somewhat contradictory results, both cases provide interesting material that has been used for both teaching students and training managers. Thus, in many lectures and management training sessions the different facets of OBA and its suitability as a tool in different types of context have been pointed out.

RESEARCH INTERVENTIONS

In the first case, Drill Inc. was interested in passing additional responsibilities to its key suppliers and, to increase its sales, the system supplier was committed to enhancing its collaboration with the OEM. The supplier was also interested in developing its costing practices and even in sharing some cost information with the OEM as an option. As part of the research collaboration, the researchers built an ABC model for the supplier. This ABC model was used for analysing the product profitability of sixteen pilot products manufactured for the OEM. The ABC model therefore formed the basis for applying OBA. In the OBA process itself, the most critical element was the meeting where the books were opened to the OEM and, in terms of research interventions, the researchers had the responsibility for co-ordinating the actual event. At the beginning of that meeting, all the participants agreed on the accounting principles used in the cost analyses and on the target values for the supplier: operating profit of 10 percent, net profit of 5 percent and ROI of 10–15 percent.

When the meeting started, only the researchers knew the actual profitability distribution among the products. However prior to the meeting the participants had been asked to estimate the profitability of each of the sixteen pilot products, and the estimates are shown in Figure 7.4. Profitability based on the ABC analysis is plotted on top of the management estimates. As seen in the figure, the profitability estimates were not that accurate, which illustrates the levels of cost awareness within both the OEM and the supplier.

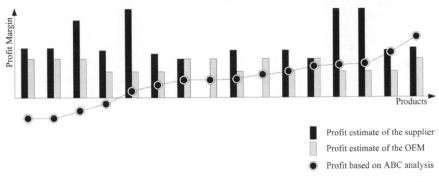

Figure 7.4   Profitability estimates of both supplier and OEM combined with calculated product profitability.

In the negotiations it became evident how important and useful it was to know how the costs of a product and, hence, the profitability of each product build up in reality. The results were taken very seriously and, in addition, all the participants were astonished at the actual profitability distribution. In the case of the supplier, its accounting department had been giving very different figures so the ABC-based results were totally surprising. The OEM's managers, on the other hand, admitted that they really had no way of analysing the costs of the products and so simply had to guess at profitability. However, the managers of the OEM were genuinely concerned about the fact that, on one hand, some of the products were unprofitable for the supplier, but on the other hand, the most profitable product had very high volumes. Thus, the evident question was:

How are we going to balance the situation?

The supplier agreed not to get rid of the unprofitable products but to look at the customer (the OEM) and the situation as a whole. It was also agreed to do some further studies before making final conclusions and defining proper actions. Thus, both parties used the cost information in a very collaborative manner.

While the first case more or less pointed out the collaborative elements usually connected to OBA, the second one turned out to be something different. At the beginning of the project relating to Excavator Inc, all the suppliers were interviewed and, based on these interviews, two of them were selected for more intensive development. As in the previous case, after some development work in cost management practices with the suppliers the time was ripe for the first exercise in IOCM. Unfortunately, things did not advance as planned. Despite attempting to use the research project as a means of increasing collaboration among the selected suppliers, suddenly the OEM decided to offer the role of a system supplier to the part supplier. In other words, the OEM made the current system supplier (system supplier

C in Figure 7.2) compete with the part supplier as to which one of the two suppliers would be the system supplier and which 'only' a part supplier. This is shown on the left of Figure 7.5.

Another issue was that, despite the attempts to increase cost awareness and information sharing within the supply network, the OEM simply asked for quotations for a particular sub-assembly from the suppliers and did not seem interested in any sort of cost information sharing. Because of this the researchers had to step in and, after some discussion, the managers of the OEM agreed that the quotations should indeed be based on comparable cost analyses and not only on price. Because there were now two suppliers making cost analyses on the same sub-assembly, the managers of the OEM wanted the researchers to create a standardised framework for the cost analyses to be included in the quotations. Furthermore, it was agreed that the researchers would be present in the meetings when the competing suppliers opened their books (that is show their quotations) to the OEM. In addition, as in the previous case, the researchers would be responsible for presenting the calculations and making sure all the participants were aware of the accounting principles used and the assumptions made during the cost analyses. Interestingly, when this decision was made, the development of cost management practices had not yet even started with the part supplier and, as a result, the development work had to be started with it immediately. However, despite this lag at the outset, the cost analyses advanced rapidly and the part supplier even finished the cost analyses needed for the quotation first.

When the open book negotiations took place with the part supplier there were, in addition to the researchers, three managers representing the part manufacturer (managing director, development manager and production manager) and five managers from the OEM. The purchasing manager was leading the OEM's delegation and, because the part manufacturer had proposed some technical innovations making the sub-assembly more efficient to manufacture, some design engineers were also present. At the beginning the costing model and the assumptions made in the framework for the cost analyses were discussed in depth, after which the focus moved on to the cost analyses themselves. In the meeting the manufacturing costs of the sub-assembly were analysed activity by activity, and the OEM's purchasing manager asked a lot of questions related to activity durations, resource consumption and the volume assumptions used in the cost analyses. Some changes were agreed for the cost analyses based on the comments and, at the end of the day, the OEM promised the part supplier that it would make the decision about the new system supplier within a month.

In contrast to the part manufacturer, the current system supplier was far less enthusiastic about collaborative cost reduction efforts. The managers did not see any means for cost reductions and so the calculations needed for the quotation were started in much less of a hurry. To illustrate its reluctance, the focus was not shifted onto the sub-assembly until at the very last moment, after the researcher had suggested it. Eventually, despite the intensive development work on costing practices, the open book negotiation with this system supplier took place one month after that with the part manufacturer. As before, the purchasing manager led the discussion from the OEM's side but this time there was only one other purchaser and no design engineers. The system supplier, on the other hand, was represented by its managing director and product manager. The standardised template used for the cost analyses meant that, this time, it was not necessary to discuss the accounting principles so the discussion could get straight to the point.

Compared with the open book negotiations with the part manufacturer, the meeting with the system supplier was a disaster. First the managers of the OEM thought there was some confusion in the resource consumption of certain activities, but this was sorted out with only a slight uneasiness in the air. However, without first talking to the researcher the system supplier had added one activity to the cost analyses. The supplier's managers had simply used the cost rate of assembly activity for it and, on top of this, its duration was about ten times higher than the real one. Whereas the researchers were supposed to be responsible of the cost model and, hence, capable of answering all possible questions, they simply had to give the floor to the system supplier's product manager because, obviously, the researchers did not have any answers. Instead of the researchers presenting a proper explanation therefore, the supplier's product manager just mumbled something. It really seemed as if the managers of the current system supplier had simply tried to ensure that the cost analyses included 'enough costs' to justify the price level. It was not a good moment for the current system supplier.

After further discussions in this meeting, the OEM's purchasing manager listed some areas where, in his opinion, the supplier's costs were too high and some changes needed to be made:

Maintenance costs of the paint shop must be reduced by 10%, pressing must be done with only one worker, finishing in half the time, mould maintenance must be reduced by at least 35%, assembly time must be reduced to 1 hour, paint consumption by half and profit by 50%.

As can be seen in the comment, the OEM's purchasing manager did not provide any ideas as to how the supplier could achieve these cost reduction targets in practice, nor how the OEM might be able to contribute to the cost reductions. The managing director of the supplier commented that they certainly could not be satisfied with the current cost level. However, when the OEM's purchasing manager asked what should be done, the managing director of the system supplier responded spontaneously:

You have not considered raising the price?

The comment was supplemented with sarcastic laughter and the managing director continued with a smile:

> *Would you like us to remove some positions [activities] or just tamper with the figures?*

The purchasing manager emphasised, again, that the figures were too high. After that, the purchasing manager pondered for a moment, hesitated then wondered:

> *Am I breaking some ethical rules here . . . ???*

Despite this slight hesitation, the OEM's purchasing manager suddenly pulled out the quotation made by the part manufacturer. With all the activities, the system supplier was more expensive. The system supplier was given a month in which it could do new cost analyses and come up with a list of proper actions to reach the target costs represented by the part supplier's quotation. This eventually created some movement within the system supplier; the manufacturing process of the sub-assembly was re-analysed and the cost-based quotation was resubmitted. In the new quotation, the system supplier was able to achieve about half of the cost reduction target. However, the cost analyses were mainly based on speculations (concerning, for example, future volumes). They lacked hard data and a concrete list of actions.

When the OEM eventually announced the result of this cost management pilot, about six months late, the decision was different from what could have been expected based on the cost analyses. The outcome of the cost management pilot is seen in Figure 7.5. The current system supplier maintained its position and, despite its relatively high cost level and unwillingness to commit to the open book practices, its level of responsibility was actually increased. The current system supplier would now take care of all the material flow related to that sub-assembly and the OEM would no longer negotiate with individual part suppliers. At the same time, the responsibility of the innovative and collaborative part manufacturer was reduced even further. Instead of attaching their parts to the frame structure coming from another part manufacturer (Part manufacturer X in Figure 7.5, which was not involved in the network project) as before, it would now only ship its part to Part manufacturer X, which would take care of the assembly work.

What can be said about the success of this development project? As far as the OEM was concerned, about 50 percent of the targeted price reduction was realised, which, when combined with the volume, was a significant annual cost reduction. In other words, the price did come down and, in a sense, the cost reduction target of the OEM was achieved. Whether the costs within the suppliers would come down as well remained a mystery.

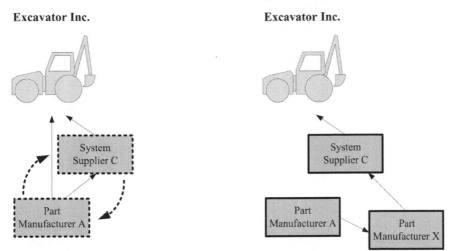

Figure 7.5   Competitive situation created by the OEM (left) and the outcome of the cost management pilot (right).

To summarise, interventions served three purposes: (1) they provided a justification for access to a specific empirical setting in the first place (the researchers were seen as resources by the managers and, hence, managers were willing to provide access), (2) within that setting, they facilitated a deepening access (immigration to the local culture) thus strengthening the role of researchers as 'members of the team' (Jönsson and Lukka 2007), and (3) by contributing to cost accounting and cost consciousness in participating organisations, they helped in creating a setting within which OBA could be practised and, most importantly, also studied. However, the researchers were mainly seen as number crunchers and, especially in the latter case, despite the active involvement in the organizations, the researchers were not let into the 'family circle of trust' though resulting in some surprising events in the research process and providing interesting data for theory contribution.

In the following chapter, the strength of the research interventions is reduced to Level 3. Interestingly, just like the one in this chapter the case discussed next also has some elements of open-book accounting in it. However, the major contribution of that one does not lie in the area of inter-organizational cost management but rather more on performance measurement and use of cost information in various decision-making situations. In that chapter, the focus shall be on the interventionist research as a tool for impacting the society surrounding academic community.

8 Interventionist Research
Impacting Society

This chapter will point out how interventionist research can have long-term implications within the target organisations, and hence can impact society aside from producing scientific output. Universities are often seen as important institutions in diffusing new technological and management innovations into the local economy, and interventionist research provides one way to enhance such knowledge diffusion. This chapter describes a case study focusing on quality costs and also the cost implications of sourcing, specifically from low-cost countries. This interventionist research process did not actually start until 2006 though the researchers had been in close collaboration with the case company's top management already since early 2000.

As pointed out by the title of this chapter, this case mainly attempts to illustrate how the interventionist research work introduces new management practices to companies and, in that way, impacts society through direct practical implications. As shown in Figure 8.1, the research interventions

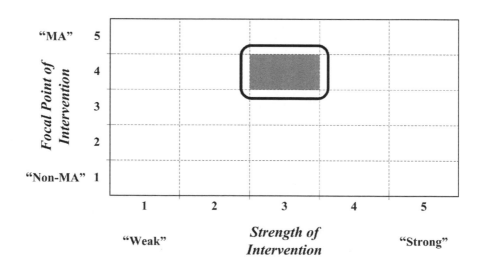

Figure 8.1 Scope and intensity of research interventions in this chapter.

undertaken were semi-strong, focusing mainly on management accounting practices.

In contrast to some of the projects discussed in earlier chapters, the project discussed here (and also the one in Chapter 9) had a well-defined project plan that was also followed quite strictly. This was because there was a relatively long history of collaboration between the case company (operating in the project business) and the responsible researcher prior to the project; both parties knew perfectly well what to expect. However, in contrast to this programmability, the project's theoretical contribution potential was not especially well identified at the outset; instead, it was just expected that something interesting would emerge.

LITERATURE ON COST OF QUALITY

Despite substantial interest in quality costing in general, there are contexts—such as project businesses—in which the effects of practical innovations on quality costing have remained quite modest (cf. Malmi et al. 2004). For example, while quality cost functions (e.g. Ittner 1996; Anderson and Sedatole 1998; Schiffauerova and Thomson 2006) form an extensive field of research, this has not produced widely applied tools or improvements in project business companies. There are also wider concerns with respect to quality costing: the variety of quality cost measures has remained rather narrow, examples of the practical use of those measures are scarce and the validity of them for decision makers has not been seriously addressed (Mandal and Shah 2002). In addition, it has been observed that surprisingly few companies even report quality-related costs (Oliver and Qu 1999). One reason for the questionable progress of quality costing may be that quality costs traditionally have been measured afterwards and, therefore, are regarded merely as 'history reports' (Oliver and Qu 1999).

In the extant literature, quality-related costs have been referred to by many names, such as quality costs, cost of quality, cost of poor quality and failure costs. In addition, many definitions of their content exist. Some definitions, such as *"the costs that would be eliminated if all workers were perfect at their jobs"* (see e.g. Rust 1995), are quite philosophical, so more analytical classifications are needed for actually measuring and analysing these costs. One approach is to divide quality-related costs into the costs of conformance and non-conformance (Crosby 1979). First, costs of conformance are costs incurred to make sure the product or service is right the first time. Costs of conformance occur when companies implement and maintain systems that aim at eliminating deficiencies, so they achieve products with perceived quality and therefore ensure conformance to quality standards. Secondly, the costs of non-conformance are incurred to correct a problem or irregularity: in other words, they compensate for non-conformance to quality standards. One way to illustrate these two concepts is that costs of conformance are incurred because poor quality *can* exist, while costs of non-conformance are incurred because poor quality *does* exist (Albright and Roth 1992).

An even finer classification of quality-related costs is the traditional PAFF model (see e.g. Feigenbaum 1961; Juran and Gryna 1993) which divides quality costs into prevention, appraisal and (internal and external) failure costs. This seems to be a framework that is cited in all studies discussing the issue of quality cost. Traditionally, it has been claimed that there is an inverse relationship between prevention and appraisal costs on the one hand, and internal and external failure costs on the other. Accordingly, there is 'economic conformance'—an optimal proportion of preventive and corrective costs (Morse 1983). However, a newer 'continuous improvement' approach argues that 'quality is free' and may be achieved through effective quality programmes without increasing investments in preventive activities to infinity (Ittner 1996; Anderson and Sedatole 1998).

When looking at quality costs (QC) from a cost modelling point of view, costs of conformance and non-conformance are very different as cost objects. While costs of conformance mainly are inherent in processes designed to deliver something, costs of non-conformance are highly unpredictable so managers usually attempt to minimise them. Basically, there must be some costs of conformance in the company to maintain quality. That may be a reason why the cost of *poor quality* especially still seems to receive more attention in the research regarding quality-related costs.

The challenge of measuring quality costs stems not only from the very concept of quality but also from certain critical considerations in the process of operationalisation. In general, a performance measure can be defined as a metric used to quantify the efficiency and/or effectiveness of an action or an end result (Neely et al. 1995), and the soundness of such a measure is typically evaluated in terms of its validity, reliability and relevance. However, unambiguous performance measures are always challenging to construct and, in real life, it is often necessary to settle for surrogate measures instead of capturing the true principles (Ijiri 1975, pp. 40–41). The use of such surrogates may increase the reliability of measurement but at the same time it perhaps weakens the validity of the measurement, as the measure moves further from the concept in which the primary interest lies.

Quality is a good example of something that is commonly measured as a surrogate ratio: the ratio of quality-related costs to sales (Mandal and Shah 2002) is a very typical QC measure used by companies for example. The principle at stake is the quality-producing ability of the organisation, which ideally would be better measured as the amount of quality-related problems in relation to the underlying burden. However, using a surrogate can be understandable for a couple of reasons. First, the surrogate is quite a feasible measure, the construction of which does not require substantial resources. Secondly, the measure gives a quick overview of the financial impact of poor quality on a business within a given period of time.

However, it leaves the connection between actual performance and its surrogate measure rather ambiguous. Suppose, for example, that one aspect of quality failures can be identified immediately after their occurrence, and these are reported as quality costs. However, another aspect of the failures goes all the way to the customer, in which case identification, reclamation, correction of the problem, and reporting of the costs may be very distant in time from the actual occurrence of the failures. This is especially true in project businesses that are characterised by a relatively low number of large deliveries. In specifying the projects, the business's inability to identify all the relevant customer needs may leave the perception of poor quality with the customer even though no actual failure occurs. Due to these issues, the quality costs per sales ratio that is traditionally used could be an invalid indicator of the phenomenon being measured.

RESEARCH OBJECTIVES AND RESEARCH SETTING

The case company discussed in this chapter is a globally operating machine construction company that delivers large production facilities and related upgrades and renovations. Such deliveries are usually organised and managed as projects. Although no substantial drifting in terms of original research questions took place during the empirical phase, a couple of new variations on the original themes were identified that seemed to include some contribution potential, both in theory and practice.

> *The objective of the case was to identify and analyse the factors that drive the quality costs in the project business, and to derive possible measurement implications. In the second phase, the aim was to identify a means of improving the cost efficiency of purchasing and sourcing operations.*

Compared with many other cases discussed in this report, the project contained many of the features of a straightforward development project. In fact, the case company co-ordinated the project in a highly disciplined fashion, with a detailed project plan and regular project meetings that gathered all the relevant people from the company together with the researchers.

The interventionist study was mainly conducted in one Finnish unit of the company; however, during the project, data covering global operations were also collected and analysed. The managers involved in the research project had wide responsibilities regarding quality issues and therefore they had access to a wide spectrum of information. In terms of the development of purchasing processes, however, the focus was on the purchasing organisation in Finland. As a consequence, the researchers only had access to the purchasing processes and related cost information of the Finnish business unit, but this nevertheless included global purchases. Figure 8.2 shows the time line of this project.

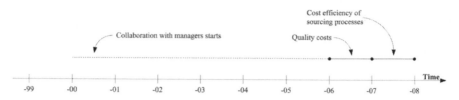

Figure 8.2   Time line of the research collaboration and the areas of main focus in the actual research project.

The first steps of collaboration between the company and CMC had been taken in around year 2000. At that time, no formal projects were launched as the collaboration mainly took the form of sparring and discussions between managers of the company and CMC. The more concrete interventions were done during a two-year period in 2006–2007. The interventions that focused on quality costing improvements were carried out in 2006, and the interventions that related to purchasing management and cost efficiency improvements were carried out in 2007.

In this case, the start of the project was a rather classic 'demand faces the supply' type of situation. As the company's development manager put it:

> There were data and there were expectations based on the data—but there was a lack of qualified and free resources. So we needed some experience and vision from outside.

This meant that a very minimal amount of actual work was required to get access to the company. It was interested in launching a couple of detailed analyses and introducing better costing tools for quality cost management and purchasing management. Because CMC had a history of collaboration with some key executives of the company in another topic area, the start of yet another mutual project was quite straightforward and natural. In fact, the first discussions about the possible project were launched in September 2005 and the project was already running in January 2006.

In short, the research setting and the research interventions had the following key characteristics. First, the company had a relatively clear (initial) agenda for the project; the company wanted to learn more about the topic and was willing to utilise external resources in the process to digest the data and help it to come up with interesting ways to analyse the existing cost data. Secondly, the researchers had a long history of working with the company's top executives before the project started, even though no formal research project had been carried out. In other words, the researchers had been important reflectors of many cost management and management accounting related issues to those executives. Finally, in addition to the clear initial agenda, the topic at the broad level seemed to provide possibilities for MA contributions, though at the beginning it was not totally clear what those contributions would be in more detail.

One distinctive feature of the project was that, in spite of the clear agenda of the company, it was particularly willing to refine the initial questions in the process of collaboration. In fact this can be seen as one of the key value drivers in interventionist collaboration, as the development manager formulated:

> *Management accounting is sometimes perceived as playing with numbers (in Finnish "numeroniilojen hommaa"). In fact it is not, but what is needed is those who ask the right questions and are willing to participate in the process of seeking answers to these questions. Interventionist MA research can well bring up themes that we don't come to think of by ourselves.*

As a result, there was mutual agreement that the research questions should be allowed to be adjusted when needed. In spite of this, no major changes were made; the adjustments were more about refining the boundaries of inquiry than actually moving them. Nevertheless, what proved to be the most important part of the management accounting contribution of the study was not exactly anticipated when the project was started.

THEORETICAL CONTRIBUTION

Even though there is a vast amount of literature focusing on quality costs, there is still room for empirical research in that area. The traditional PAFF model (see e.g. Feigenbaum 1961; Juran and Gryna 1993) is a coherent way to analyse quality costs. However, it does not really provide any practical advice on how to actually manage quality costs. In other words, there is plenty of research potential in identifying the causal relationships that explain the behaviour of quality costs, then implementing solutions in practical decision-making situations.

Because many of the publications based on the project are still in progress, the theoretical potential of the case has not yet been fully tested. Something can be argued nevertheless (Varila et al. 2007). The study provided an empirical setting for focusing on the possibilities and challenges of quality costing. The feasibility of both *ex-ante* quality costing and more traditional *ex-post* quality measures was elaborated. Hence, the case extended and refined the existing research on quality costing, which is especially poor on empirical examples of *ex-ante* measurement. Relying on the empirical data, the case demonstrated that average quality costs can be roughly predicted based on various indicators of volume and business/customer novelty. This could not only help in setting realistic targets but could also start a series of preventive actions. The study suggested that proactive quality cost information on risky customers and market areas, difficult projects, failure-prone products, weak suppliers and other bottlenecks should be delivered to various sections of the order-delivery process to help in predicting quality risks and preventing them from occurring.

In addition to its theoretical contribution in terms of quality costs, the case also motivated a more general discussion about the validity aspect of the ratio type of performance measurement (Suomala et al. 2007). The context of quality cost measurement in the project businesses typical of the case company was used as an illustrative example of the challenges that might be faced when striving to maintain validity in practice. However, in addition to identification of the challenges, the case also provided some possible ways to overcome these challenges. Essentially, the study pointed out that some surrogate ratios (such as quality costs/sales) have become so established that their validity has not been seriously considered at the conceptual level, even though they may not be valid measures of the concepts that are of primary interest.

The study highlighted that validity is always constructed into the measures used in a given context, and threats to validity may be faced at any step from defining the concept and operationalising the definition to actual measurement, although operationalisation (as a specific step in the process of creating a measure) was noticed to be the most challenging step. Another important conclusion based on the study was that threats to validity seem to arise in relation to ratios if the causal relations between the numerator and denominator are not properly identified, or if they are especially difficult to conceptualise. It was also found that validity is a highly context-specific issue, so the requirements for the causal relationship may depend on the user of the measure.

MANAGERIAL IMPLICATIONS

From the company's perspective, the research project was able to provide valuable answers to the initial questions. The researchers developed a model that is able to estimate the quality costs in the future (rolling forecast) at a given level of uncertainty. The model has been now empirically validated over several years and the company has been active in utilising it—for instance in discussions between top managers and quality managers. It is seen as a good tool in explicating concerns about and means of managing the effects of quality failures.

Whereas the theoretical contribution of this research project was mainly positioned in the area of quality costs and performance measurement, there were also several interesting outcomes that could be seen as practical contributions in terms of purchasing management. On the basis of development work done as part of the research collaboration, purchasing managers have adopted a number of principles for co-ordinating their sourcing processes. For example, the project's cost modelling was used to show the investment cost needed when searching for and auditing a new supplier in a low cost country. As a result, purchasing managers increasingly do not just look at the purchase price but also have a better understanding of the impacts of different cost components in such a context. The project, in all, has contributed to a more holistic view of the supplier selection process. Another example is an analysis of how the price seems to behave in different item categories as a function of different design parameters. Using statistical tools, the researchers were able to discover factors that affect the price of various sourced components. This has facilitated control over purchase prices and has reduced the company's reliance on the tacit knowledge of individuals in the sourcing department.

RESEARCH INTERVENTIONS

The main contact in the case company was a top executive interested in doing a PhD in industrial management, focusing on management of R&D activities. Despite many collaborative tasks at the beginning of the century, it was not until the autumn of 2005 that the researchers and the particular executive (who by this time had become responsible for quality management) started to talk about a more formal, interventionist research collaboration. Nevertheless after this the process advanced very rapidly, and in early 2006 the research project was going forward at full speed.

Table 8.1 reports the key phases—or steps—within the research collaboration. In the first year, the researchers spent most of their time conducting quantitative analyses focusing on different aspects of quality and quality costs. In line with the key question that had motivated the study—how do our quality costs behave and what drives them?—the analyses focused on the determinants of quality failure (either internal or external) and related cost effects.

A lot of costing data were analysed in order to identify and classify the drivers of quality costs. Quality cost histories covering several years were studied incident by incident in order to establish a sound basis for conclusions. During a two month period the field researcher spent several weeks at the site, familiarising himself with the data and explicating more qualitative interpretations of it. After several months of analysis and discussions with company representatives, the focus was shifted to the construction of measures. This can be regarded as a more analytical and theoretical phase which was, however, supported by discussions with managers. The final set of interventions consisted of presentations and training sessions aiming at dispersion of accumulated knowledge within the organisation.

After the first year the focus was shifted from Part A (Quality) to Part B (Purchasing). This move can be interpreted as a 'call option' because, prior

Table 8.1   The Key Steps of the Research Project

Step	Data, tools & methods	Time
PART A: QUALITY		
1. Start & familiarising	Meetings, company documents	01–02/2006
2. Literature review on QC	Journals, books	02–03/2006
3. Analysis of quality data	Quality database	03–05/2006
4. Detailed analysis of case environment	Interviews, surveys	06–08/2006
5. Introduction of quality measures	Quantitative analysis (Access DB)	08–11/2006
6. Education and presentations	Reports on project	11–12/2006
PART B: PURCHASING		
1. Start	Discussions	02/2007
2. Analysis of purchasing data	Purchasing database	02–04/2007
3. Interviews of personnel	Interviews, discussions	03/2007
4. Delivery project case A and B	Documents, interviews	06–09/2007
5. Reporting	Reports on project	10–11/2007

to the study, parts A and B were not designed as a package: rather it was accepted that the decision to move to part B would be based on good results being achieved in part A. Promising results, especially from the company's perspective, meant there was an interest in carrying on with collaboration. The purchasing manager, who had followed part A to some extent, came up with the idea that the tools employed in part A could actually be put into practice in the domain of purchasing as well.

The second year did not need much of an introduction because the researchers were already quite familiar with the environment. In fact, the second year focused very much on quantitative analysis of a new data-set, this time relating to prices and the costs of purchasing. In addition, the CMC researchers conducted two in-depth analyses on purchases and global sourcing around delivery projects.

Throughout the project, quantitative analysis of existing data was combined with acquiring new qualitative and quantitative data using both interviews and survey tools. This concerned both quality data and purchasing data. The interventions made in the project can be classified as semi-strong because the work did not only result in conducted analyses and associated reports but also in operative performance measures and databases that company representatives have been using operatively since the project was closed. Therefore it is fair to say that the interventionist work has left a clear mark on the organisation and it has directly contributed to its processes of cost management (in quality and purchasing). Another dimension to consider regarding the strength of contribution is the research process itself. Over the (roughly two-year) process the researchers spent about 350–400 hours on site. During these visits the researchers got to know many of the key people in the organisation and, thanks to their in-depth analyses of the existing quality and cost data, they became experts on the many systems and databases inside the company.

Several reasons for participation in the research project with the case company can be identified. First, empirical work in quality costing in the machine construction sector (a project-based business) is especially limited. Secondly, purchasing and sourcing are the key success factors in businesses that resemble the case company, where purchases are about 65 percent of sales. The challenge of low-cost sourcing and international project deliveries creates new pressures on existing suppliers, not only in the case company but also in many other industries. For example, when projects are being delivered in developing markets the OEMs often wish to source various components locally but from the same suppliers that they use domestically. Thus, existing suppliers should (in theory) follow the OEMs and become international, but they hold back as they do not have the competencies and how far the OEMs will help them is not self- evident. As mentioned previously, there is a lack of knowledge about the real cost and profit implications of low-cost sourcing and the total cost of ownership when sourcing from low-cost countries. All this means pressure for MA development. Thirdly, both the data and the access were expected to be valuable as the executives involved in the project had influential positions inside the company. Finally, the collaboration was expected to be straightforward as CMC already had connections with the key executives for several years.

To summarise, the role of interventionist researchers was (1) to analyse existing data and produce conclusions based on that, (2) to collect new data and evoke discussions inside the organisation and (3) to establish feasible costing tools that could help the company's managers in improving their cost consciousness and cost efficiency. In other words, the researchers were mainly perceived as external experts with a certain set of skills and abilities. However, considering the nature of collaboration between the company and CMC prior to the project, it is likely that the personal qualities of the researchers played a role as well. Interventions provided the company with the required resources for data mining and data analysis, so they enabled interesting learning opportunities for company managers. For the researchers, the interventionist approach enabled 'the deepest possible' access. One contact person in the company reported that, after the project had been running for about six months, one of the employees had wondered "who is the new guy that works for us . . ." referring to one of the researchers.

This chapter has attempted to point out the likely 'social impact' of interventionist research. As the discussion on managerial implications pointed out, there were plenty of practical contributions, especially for the particular case company. In many interventionist research projects (at least in Finland), the companies partly fund research and, as a result, they usually expect something in return. Thus the companies expect that researchers will provide them with new ways of doing things and, in a sense, will help with diffusion of best practice to the local society. It would be tempting to ask whether participation in the implementation of such practices is really the role or responsibility of the researchers—should they not be more interested in producing theoretical contributions? However, one should also ask whether such participation does any harm. In many cases, it is difficult to identify theoretical contributions and, more importantly, relevant theoretical contributions. Thus should it not be a good thing that a research project at least provides some benefits to the case organisation? Is this not better than running a project that does not result in significant practical contributions, but at the same time, does not provide any relevant theoretical contribution either? One could even claim that in order to ensure that research work (using whatever research approach) provides results with pragmatic relevance, the results of the research should be reflected with practitioners. This is inherent in interventionist research when working intensively with practitioners.

Despite pointing out to the potential social impacts of management accounting research, our attempt is not to say that all research should be done using interventionist research approach. On the contrary, interventionist research is just one tool in the researcher's toolbox that has it pros and cons. The next chapter discusses how this research method plays its own role in line with other research methods.

9 Research Intervention as Part of a Toolbox

The case in Chapter 6 focused on product costing and pointed out the significance of the life cycle perspective when analysing product profitability. This chapter discusses a series of shorter projects focusing on the issue of life cycle costing and life cycle profitability. These projects were carried out with different organisations, and they constitute a cluster of studies contributing to the topic of long term cost and profitability management. In this chapter, the focus is on projects started after 2003. In many respects, these were still underway in 2009.

This chapter shows how interventionist research can be part of a researcher's toolbox providing just one additional way to increase knowledge and understanding of the phenomenon under investigation. In addition, compared with the other cases, the intensity of research interventions discussed in this chapter can be classified the lowest, as shown in Figure 9.1.

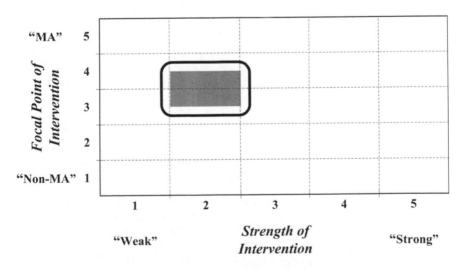

Figure 9.1 The scope and intensity of research interventions in this cluster of research projects.

While the cases discussed thus far in Part II have focused on relatively strong research interventions, this chapter looks at more modest interventions. The weaker intensity of the research interventions is mainly explained by the fact that the research projects are shorter compared than the ones discussed up to now. When looking at the focal point of research interventions in this chapter, the interventions fall somewhere between those focusing on MA and non-MA. Furthermore, the research topics and questions did not result from iterative empirical work, as was the case in many of the previous examples. On the contrary, the starting points of the cases were closely associated with the results of quantitative survey studies on life cycle costing. In other words, based on the prior surveys, there were many presuppositions that guided the empirical work from the outset.

EXISTING LITERATURE ON LIFE CYCLE COSTING

Life cycle costing (LCC) should be seen as a costing perspective in which attention is directed towards the total costs that occur during the life (or existence) of an accounting object. The accounting object can be a customer, a product or some sort of asset (see for example Asiedu and Gu 1998; Booth 1994; Woodward 1997; Jackson and Ostrom 1980). When practising LCC, the costs can also be analysed from many perspectives. For example, the viewpoint of the product's supplier may include analysis of the impact of after-sales (as we saw in Chapter 6). The user or owner of a product may be interested in maintenance and usage related costs in addition to purchase price. Even more broadly, society's point of view in LCC may reveal many indirect consequences, say on the environment, that can be associated with the accounting object. In all, the notion of LCC implies that the total costs/profits of an object can be influenced (Markeset and Kumar 2004), but in order to do that the interrelations between the various costs have to be understood. A decrease in costs relating to one aspect (for example, using cheaper but heavier material when manufacturing a passenger car) can lead to an increase in costs in another aspect (higher fuel consumption). Thus, to avoid partial optimisation, the costs must be studied with regard to the whole.

When adopting the user's perspective, LCC is very closely related to the idea of total cost of ownership (TCO) (see Ellram 1995; Wouters et al. 2005). The basis of both ideas is to strive to formulate a holistic view of the economic consequences of a decision. This means that, in the context of purchasing or capital investment, costing has two broad agendas:

- *Ex-ante*: estimating the future costs on the life cycle basis and
- *Ex-post*: monitoring the costs incurred during the life cycle

The rationale for TCO and LCC in general is that a significant part of total costs consists of other elements than the purchase price. In this sense, holistic cost-consciousness calls for understanding of life cycle costs (Velasquez and Suomala 2009). Implementation of LCC or TCO is, however, known to be difficult (Lindholm and Suomala 2005); it easily leads to highly complicated and laborious analyses of cause and effect. However, when implementing LCC at a company level and monitoring acquisition and operational costs in more detail, management can expose the cost structure and cost behaviour of a particular investment and, as a result, reveal several interesting causalities. For example, when maintenance costs are monitored at a machine level, it is possible to identify when the maintenance costs of a certain machine rapidly increase, indicating the need for re-investment (Lindholm and Suomala 2007).

RESEARCH OBJECTIVES AND RESEARCH SETTING

Whereas the collaboration with the host organisation described in Chapter 7 started in the late 1990s, involvement in life cycle costing (LCC) is somewhat more recent. With regards to CMC, research work around the topic started with a couple of present state analyses in 2003. The idea of these analyses was to better understand what is going on in Finland and, more broadly, in Europe in terms of LCC. The idea for such analyses was brought up by a consulting and engineering company, which happened to approach CMC with this issue. The company wanted to know more about the current applications of LCC in order to be able to develop new business models around LCC consultation.

The first present state analysis was conducted in the Finnish machine construction and railway transportation industry in 2003 and 2004 (reported in Järvinen et al. 2004). The aim was to identify both suppliers' and buyers' experiences and perceptions on LCC, and the significance of life cycle costs in general. Companies representing different positions in supply chains were interviewed and, using these interviews, a questionnaire was developed for further empirical inquiry. The questionnaire was further employed in 2004 with a larger sample of European manufacturers and operators in the railway transportation industry (Järvinen 2004; Lindholm and Suomala 2005).

The present state analyses did not include any interventionist elements in them. However they raised interest in the topic and, consequently, several interventionist research projects followed the early empirical work, as illustrated in Figure 9.2. The projects with the dashed lines can be seen as interventionist research projects whereas the LCC in Finland project (at the top of the figure) refers to a broader research project with only some interventionist elements in it.

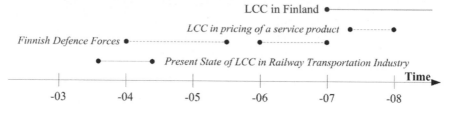

Figure 9.2   Research projects focusing on LCC practices.

As seen in Figure 9.2, two interventionist research projects were carried out with Finnish Defence Forces (FDF) over the years 2004–2007. In the first project, the focus was on modelling the life cycle costs of one weapon system in order to develop long term cost monitoring and management processes in the case organisation. The role of the researchers was to construct the model and identify the required cost elements and assignment rules. In addition, the researchers actively instructed the gathering process of cost data, mainly carried out by representatives of the organisation. The aim of the second research project with FDF became something that actually should have preceded the first project: it focused on clarifying the information needs and decision context characteristics experienced by the decision-makers when buying various physical assets (weapon systems). In this project, the main intervention was the construction and introduction of a conceptual model connecting the decision-making situation with life cycle costs.

A while after completion of the second interventionist project with FDF, a representative of a large manufacturing company contacted CMC. He had heard that CMC had developed expertise in LCC modelling and he wanted to discuss collaboration in a project focusing on cost estimation and cost-based pricing of a maintenance service product. The initial discussion led to collaboration between this company and CMC during 2007–2008. The role of CMC was to introduce scenario-based cost simulations using the principles and tools that had been mainly developed during the first project with FDF. Together these projects facilitated CMC in strengthening its expert role in terms of LCC which, eventually, helped the research team leader to receive the status of research fellow funded by Academy of Finland.

The description above attempts to illustrate the degree of fragmentation in the research projects and the multitude of organisations involved in this research stream. However despite the fragmented structure of the research collaboration and the lack of a long-term orientation such as characterised the other cases discussed thus far, all these projects shared the objective to increase both theoretical and practical understanding of LCC.

> *The objective of this research stream has been to increase the understanding of LCC, its applicability in general and the use of it amongst Finnish companies in particular. In this study, the focus was mainly on*

LCC as a means to understand the long-term cost implications of an asset to its user.

One must also point out that this research stream does not only include the research collaboration and research projects with the organisations mentioned in Figure 9.2. On the contrary, this area of research has had linkages to other research projects, most notably to the one discussed in the Chapter 6. However, as noted previously, this chapter focuses primarily on the three interventionist case studies shown in Figure 9.2.

THEORETICAL CONTRIBUTION

Concerning the theoretical contribution of this research stream, in terms of the present state analyses the results showed that real-life applications of LCC were extremely rare, although some activities related to LCC could be detected during the different phases of the sourcing process. However, it was uncommon to systematically monitor the components of assets' life cycle costs during the active life cycle of those items. Companies were mainly monitoring those maintenance costs that could be traced with reasonable effort—not necessarily those that are important. However, even regarding these traceable maintenance costs, cumulated cost data was seldom analysed and utilised afterwards. The results of the extended survey were in line with the domestic study: there are prejudices towards LCC that are mainly based on the uncertainty present in *ex-ante* costing. In addition, many companies see that the pace of development in their business is too rapid for meaningful *ex-ante* LCC (Lindholm and Suomala 2005). Throughout the companies, the practice of LCC was very much dependent on the possible enthusiasm of single individuals. LCC was not found to be a fully diffused company policy or a strong cultural feature anywhere.

These survey findings provided a very interesting starting point for interventionist studies aiming at increased understanding of the practical challenges connected with collecting adequate data and practising long-term cost management in environments with uncertainty. In a sense this interventionist study, in contrast to many others discussed in this report, started with fairly well-developed pre-understanding based on the survey study. When looking at the theoretical contribution of these interventionist projects, the first project with the FDF showed that the characteristics of LCC and the results achieved by using it evolve significantly from the beginning of a product's life cycle to its disposal. In other words, from the theoretical point of view, it was argued that the 'LCC' at the beginning of a product's life cycle is something quite different compared with the 'LCC' at the end of it. Naturally, the interventionist research process enabled an illustration of how a number of practical issues, such as availability and quality of input data, are connected with the decision-making needs of different stakeholders (Lindholm and Suomala 2007).

In all, costing interventions within the participating organisations forced the researchers to face up to the obstacles of LCC observed previously. This experience of 'practising theory' both verified some of these obstacles and showed how relatively simple costing techniques can be utilised in learning from existing data and improving organisational cost consciousness. Furthermore, later LCC applications in relation to service pricing showed LCC's potential in areas in which its usage has not yet been widely reported. Service businesses in general, and in this case a comprehensive maintenance service in particular, result in resource consumption which needs to be managed in a longer term. However, the publication of this part of our empirical work is still in progress.

MANAGERIAL IMPLICATIONS

Managerial implications of the survey study initiated by the consulting and engineering company are not fully visible for us. This is because they mainly relate to the actions of the company, in addition to facilitating the development of LCC research in CMC. Based on the survey, it was observed that, given the relatively undeveloped LCC practices in the field, there is indeed some potential for consulting and policy development. However, the impact of these observations on the actions of the particular consulting and engineering company, or on those of other actors, to our knowledge has not been substantial. A few years after the collaboration, a CMC researcher met one of the managers of the consulting and engineering company. When the researcher asked about their possible new LCC projects, the manager responded:

> . . . *well, we have done something [related to LCC], but not much.*

When looking at the interventionist work with FDF, more practical implications can be identified. It was shown that the major obstacles related to the data gathering needed for LCC can be overcome—if there is the commitment to do so. In addition, when attempting to apply LCC it is important to define what the cost information will be used for. In the context of FDF, there are many alternative systems that can be purchased, but at the same time, there is not enough funding for them to be effectively utilised. Thus, even rough estimates when making selections on purchased products or technologies could be sufficient in terms of finding out whether that considered product is feasible for the organisation. However, on some occasions, LCC seems to be a more powerful tool for selecting between major technological platforms rather than suppliers or products.

The uncertainties inherent in estimating the cost of alternative products make it perhaps too difficult to reliably base product or supplier selection on LCC—especially if the cost analyses are made by the buyer, which does not possess detailed technical knowledge on the product. In those cases, it is understandable that the differences in the average estimated costs are deemed insignificant compared with the uncertainties within these calculations. Most importantly, according to our observations, LCC should not be directly used as a control technology but rather as a learning tool (cf. Chapman 1997). Through long-term exercises with LCC, an organisation can gradually learn to understand cause-and-effect relationships in relation to its costs. This would eventually facilitate, for instance, better timing of decisions related to the acquisition, disposal or upgrading of defence material. In particular, the second project with FDF pointed out how important it is to establish internally consistent practices on costing. Consistency refers to the requirement that costing considerations are not just *ad hoc* exercises but are part of management and co-ordination from RFQ (request for quotation) preparation to eventual disposal. By proposing a template for evaluating quotations in which life cycle costs play a role, the study discussed whether and how it would be possible to proceed towards such an organisational culture where long term cost effects are both discussable and of interest at different levels in the organisation.

With respect to another case company, managerial implications are fairly explicit. The motivation of the company for the collaboration was connected to the pricing of a maintenance service product. The company was interested in finding out cost-based boundaries and risks should be taken into account when setting the price. As a result of the project, the service product was analysed in detail and the resources associated with the provision of service were identified. In other words, the company reached the main objectives set for the project and could utilise the results in the pricing process.

RESEARCH INTERVENTIONS

It is known in the extant literature that the military sector is one of the pioneers in LCC, and this was also one of the reasons for the researchers to approach the Finnish Defence Forces (FDF). It was quickly learned that FDF might indeed be interested in developing their LCC practices. According to the preliminary signals from the organisation, some LCC models had been developed but these had remained rather theoretical exercises. Thus an interventionist research project was set up, and the project focused on the development of feasible and expedient LCC models in the context of FDF.

Compared with the other cases discussed in this report, the starting point of this research project was rather different. In other cases, there had been, right from the beginning, clear pragmatic objectives for the research interventions whereas the theoretical contribution potential had been more of a mystery. In this case, the survey had pointed out interesting issues to study and there was also an organisation with a clear interest in the topic. However, compared with the other cases, this time the study did not involve any direct funding from the case organisation (FDF). On the contrary, the research project was funded by a foundation supporting academic studies in the military sector. Thus, the discussion regarding such an interventionist research project had started with the general administration of FDF and all they could do was to point out a few possible partners inside the organisation who might possibly be willing to engage in more intensive collaboration. Thus, a practical problem was that, initially, CMC did not have sufficient direct connections with the FDF organisation and, hence, could not identify a suitable partner to actually do the interventionist research with. However, after a number of discussions and presentations about the scope of the research, it was agreed that one unit of FDF that was responsible for certain weapon systems would co-operate in order to develop LCC modelling that was suitable in their context.

During a six-month period, a model for calculating the life cycle costs related to a weapon system was developed and all the related retrospective cost data was gathered (see Lindholm and Suomala 2007). The role of the researchers was to construct the model and to identify required cost elements and assignment rules. As part of that process, participation and observation were needed in order to understand the context at hand and gather the basic information needed for building the costing model. In addition to participation, interviews and group interviews were also used for collecting the cost data. Some of the cost data was gathered by the case organisation, but the researchers were actively instructing and managing that data gathering process.

One of the main objectives of the case organisation was to increase cost awareness, that is to understand what is the 'cost image' of their assets in the long term. As a result, it was important to discuss the findings with the employees. In early 2005, the results were presented to representatives of FDF. The project got positive feedback from all levels, but individuals had different interpretations as to which part of the work had been the most valuable. Some regarded the LCC modelling techniques applied as the most important component, whereas others perceived the attention towards long term cost effects in general as the most valuable part. Within the discussions that took place during those meetings, it was concluded that LCC practices could be applied with a reasonable effort in FDF. However, it remained open how FDF would actually proceed with the matter.

Interestingly, about a year later, FDF contacted CMC again to point out that there was a need to make an effort to connect LCC more intensively with the process of sourcing in order to promote its utilisation in the organisation. This led to the second project with FDF. This time the contact represented the part of the organisation where the actual work would be done. In this second project, the main intervention was the construction and introduction of a conceptual model connecting the decision-making situations related to sourcing and life cycle costs. The process related to this lasted a little less than one year, and it consisted of several interviews, workshops and analytical work on the basis of the organisation's process models and target-setting descriptions for sourcing activities. It was, however, fairly autonomous and independent of the organisation. This is the very reason that the strength of interventions during the project were categorised as relatively weak compared to the first project and many other projects discussed in this report. As a whole, the project provided the researchers with a good opportunity first to observe the culture related to sourcing in the organisation, secondly to analyse the potential of a management accounting approach in this context and, thirdly, to participate in the organisational discussions that were about developing the management and measurement of sourcing and its effects.

Soon after completion of the second interventionist research project with FDF, a company wanted to engage in a project focusing on cost estimation and cost-based pricing of a maintenance service product. As a result of these discussions, a short-term research project was started. The role of CMC was to introduce scenario-based cost simulations using the principles and tools that had been developed in the research project with FDF. It turned out that the cost modelling approach, which was first developed for fixed asset cost management and sourcing support, could be reasonably easily adjusted to support a rather different process. Similar to the other cases discussed in this chapter, the research interventions relied heavily on the expert role of the researcher, who was mainly supporting the process and guiding the company's people in the cost modelling process. The company representatives were mainly responsible for cost modelling and data gathering.

As a direct result of this project, a reasonably comprehensive cost estimate regarding the product in focus was produced. The cost estimate was very interesting, but as in many other cases, the discussions with the managers within the company turned out to be even more interesting. Some of these discussions led in a fascinating direction: it was discovered that the maintenance product, the pricing of which was the primary interest of the project, should probably be carefully fitted into different customer segments in order to be able to effectively support the company's profitability development. In other words, a concern was raised that by straightforwardly selling this product to all interested customers, the company may actually harm customer profitability in certain cases. Unfortunately, the company's awareness of its customer-level profitability was very limited and did not support profitability-based segmentation. As a consequence, it was decided that the next target for intervention would be the development of a customer profitability analysis framework. This resulted in a project a couple of years later, which is not reported here. Thus, in a sense, the research collaboration focusing on a more specific topic also forced the managers to start working on the basics of profitability management.

To conclude, the interventions in this research stream connected to LCC were initiated by a couple of interesting empirical findings. The first was the paradox between the potential of LCC and its lack of utilisation, raised by questionnaire and interview studies in the field. Together with these findings, a lucky coincidence led CMC to investigate LCC in real life settings. By their nature, the interventions were attempts to utilise LCC in various decision-making contexts in different kinds of organisations. Although this series of studies—with a sort of theoretical replication idea—had not been planned in advance, it nevertheless provided a good opportunity to learn about issues that can help in matching the costing tool with the demands present in real-life settings. Without going any more deeply into the theoretically interesting findings of these studies, it can be said that LCC can be much simpler, less resource intensive, and thus more useful and expedient compared with the typical prejudices to which it is subject (see Järvinen 2004).

Importantly, the last study discussed here demonstrated one of the strengths of interventionist management accounting research: a well-grounded shift of focus during the research process (in this case from LCC to customer profitability analysis), which can sometimes tell us much about the applicability and context-specificity of management accounting applications. Furthermore, when it comes to intensity of the researcher–practitioner collaboration, the stream of LCC studies represents almost the whole range of possibilities. At one end, the actual intervention was delivered by means simply a couple of meetings and discussion; at the other end, the interventions required intensive month-long collaboration between representatives of the organisation and CMC. In the end, the smaller projects conducted over the years have helped CMC to build expertise in LCC and, eventually, has helped CMC to get funding from the Academy of Finland in order to study LCC practices (and long-term cost awareness in general) in Finland.

As with products or technologies, research into different phenomena tends to have a life cycle. In many cases, a new phenomenon is first studied at a conceptual and shallow level until more profound empirical inquiries are done. Along such a trajectory, interventionist research is just one option. Thus interventionist research should not be seen as an alternative, but on the contrary, simply as one additional tool in the researcher's toolbox. The interventionist research projects—even though they were the least intensive compared with the other projects discussed in this report—nevertheless provided nice *emic* level understanding of the challenges and potential of LCC in real life contexts and, at the same time, indicated that LCC, in the end, can be carried out using relatively simple tools.

Part III

Lessons Learned

10 Analysing the Research Projects

Part II illustrated and discussed the features of selected interventionist studies and pointed out some of the findings and contributions related to those studies. Whereas Part II focused mainly on descriptions of the cases, Part III will take a more analytical approach to the research interventions described.

THE POSSIBILITIES OF INTERVENTIONIST RESEARCH

In all, the analysed studies demonstrated the versatility of the interventionist approach to management accounting research: interventions may facilitate studies focusing on the practical meanings and impacts of relatively new MA technologies that are not yet widely diffused to companies; the idea of the intervening researcher may help in getting and building access to practice (at different organisational levels); and the empirical research process can serve as a vehicle for explicating something perceived as invisible, non-discussable or ambiguous ('opening black-boxes'). Furthermore, aside from being a research approach aiming at theoretical contributions, interventionist research can be seen as a programme that inherently addresses the practical utility of academic research and supports collaboration between academia and industry.

Despite the benefits we associate with the approach, interventionist research should not be seen as the sole ideal but rather as a part of the researcher's toolbox. As rewarding as IV research may be at its best, it is important to understand that different questions call for different research strategies and designs. Over the life cycle of a topic, interventionist research may well shed light on emerging issues but it may also be helpful in conducting 'reality-checks' in parallel with, say, large-scale quantitative studies and experimental designs during the later stages of the life cycle. Finally, as the practice of management accounting is to a great extent embedded in the operations and activities of real-life organisations—not only in control or finance functions—interventionist research aimed at contributing to MA may also utilise non-accounting interventions.

The last point is perhaps worth some further clarification. The logic is that, despite the boundaries of academic disciplines, many kinds of intervention may catalyst management accounting considerations within the organisation and thus create fruitful opportunities for understanding the roles and meanings of management accounting in real environments. This is a great opportunity for management accounting research in general, which—in our view—is not thus far fully exploited. The embedded nature of management accounting also means that individual studies may potentially contribute to many domains. Even within our sample, not all of the conducted studies contributed only to management accounting; they also contributed to other domains such as engineering management, quality management and management in general. However, taking full advantage of the multi-disciplinary possibilities may call for versatile research teams or partnerships instead of individual researchers, even during the empirical phase.

In the spirit of Labro and Tuomela (2003), with regard to constructive research in management accounting we mobilise these conducted studies through reflective analysis of methodological suggestions for researchers seeking to employ interventionist approaches in their own empirical inquiries. In this section, we will first discuss access and acts of intervention in terms of the research process, and then we will address eight key lessons learned on the basis of our retrospective analysis.

As Jönsson and Lukka (2007) aptly pointed out, an interventionist researcher has to be able to straddle two worlds during the research process. Access to the *emic* (or insider) world is pursued during the empirical phase in particular, while the *etic* (more outsider) stance is required in reflection and for deriving broader implications based on the empirical evidence. The rationale for the above analysis is already thoroughly discussed in the literature (ibid.). Our experience, however, can still provide some explicit observations how this requirement can be realised. Namely, we identify several patterns of straddling, each of them having distinct explanations and implications.

In terms of intervention strength, the projects were divided into several classes (see Chapter 3 for the analytical framework). Overall, it seems that the question of intervention strength cannot be reduced to a dichotomy including only "strong" or "modest" types of IV research. In reality, the strength of research interventions can vary a lot. On the one hand, being present in the right place can already be interpreted as an act of intervention (Jönsson and Lukka 2007), but on the other hand forceful introduction of new accounting tools or techniques is obviously a research intervention. Thus, the acts of intervention between just being present and forceful implementation form a continuum that has to be taken into account when analysing the strength of intervention.

In our view, there is no such thing as an absolute insider or outsider; rather, reality may be understood as layers. In this respect, we are dealing with ontological considerations (cf. Burrel and Morgan 1979): some phenomena may be basically visible for all, whereas some others may be observed only by rare individuals. Thus, instead of being an outsider or an insider, a researcher may actually be 'some sort of an insider' with rather limited visibility over layers of reality (shown at the top in Figure 10.1). There might not be intrinsic value associated with any particular level of nativeness but the depth of access should be nonetheless acknowledged during the inquiry. A further question is whether the strength of intervention and the depth of access are correlated. Our evidence thus far is limited in this respect, but it seems that a straightforward connection should not be expected: strong interventions are likely to be possible even without native status. At the level of researcher, a good reputation and acknowledged expertise may facilitate strong interventions which would not otherwise be realisable without deep immigration into the organisation.

Our experience shows that the depth of access should also be interpreted as a function of time. During the research process there may be many episodes of straddling between *etic* and *emic* level of varying lengths of time (solid line in the curve in the middle of Figure 10.1). Furthermore, some of our projects (see especially Chapters 4 and 5) demonstrate how access actually develops during the empirical process (dotted line in the middle of Figure 10.1). This is mainly because of increasing trust and perceived value within the collaboration and between parties.

The final issues brought up here arise from a combination of two dimensions of access: the depth of access and the length of access (see at the bottom of Figure 10.1). In our view, successful interventions (success mainly

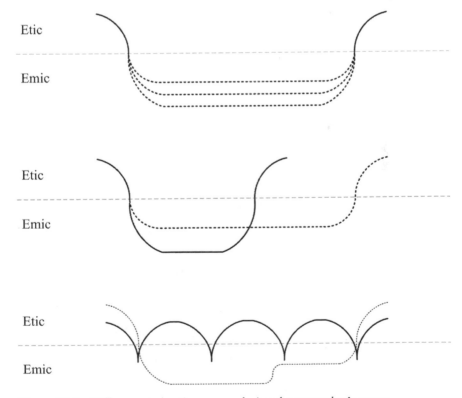

Figure 10.1 Different perspectives on analysing the researcher's access.

being interpreted as perceived value by the participating organisation) may indeed drive them both.

The research question, with its ontological underpinnings, largely determines whether depth or length of access should be pursued. In other words, these two dimensions are alternatives rather than substitutes. The depth of access relates mainly to the ontological selection. The length of access has a connection to the richness and time frame of the gathered data. Again, it depends on the research question as to what is necessary and sufficient.

INTERVENTIONIST MA RESEARCH—LESSONS LEARNED

The eight lessons learned from the described projects are categorised under three broad headings: first, we identify some general issues that surround IV research; secondly, we identify research design issues that should be acknowledged when applying IV research or considering the possibility of applying it; thirdly, we identify issues relating to the actual research process in doing IV research. The following list includes these lessons in short:

General issues:

1. An intervention is used for building a research setting—not for building the research question *per se*.
2. IV research has potential to provide researchers with a means of creating a real and direct impact outside the academic world (impact on society).
3. IV research should not only be seen as an approach for collecting empirical data but also as a vehicle for creating sustainable relations between academia and different industries.

Research design issues:

4. The idea of the intervening researcher can be utilised in getting true (*emic*) access and acceptance within the host organisation.
5. Interventionist work may be one of the rare available research tools for studying issues that are 'bubbling under': issues that have not yet been extensively explored by real life organisations.
6. IV research can be regarded as a specific tool in a 'methodological toolbox' that should be fitted into a researcher's capabilities and into the possibilities occurring during a research topic's life cycle.

Data collection and processing related issues:

7. IV research can be used as a mechanism for opening black boxes of organisational activities and, when applied with sufficient rigour, as

a means of avoiding the problems connected with failing to recollect and/or hiding undesired behaviour.

8. The act of intervention can be used for validating results immediately during the process of research. This supports both the relevance and efficiency of theory production.

Let us now look at each one of these eight issues in more detail. Note that the sequence of presenting these does not imply any order of priority.

"An intervention is used for building a research setting—not for building the research question *per se*"

This is the very reason why many interventions grounded in disciplines other than management accounting (such as engineering) can be helpful in management accounting research. In general, an intervention serves as a vehicle for change. The change, in turn, provides interesting outlooks for management accounting researchers. However, it should be understood that this logic seems not to be applicable to interventionist research in all disciplines, rather that it relates to a central idiosyncrasy of MA—namely to its plethora of interfaces with different organisational phenomena.

Despite the fact that the actual research question in interventionist management accounting research may be only indirectly linked with the intervention (such as in Chapters 4 and 5), it is necessary for the link between the two not to be artificial. Consider an intervention, such as developing a modular architecture for an ETO product in Chapter 4, and the related target of interest or research question, such as how a shift in the business logic (mobilised by the modular architecture) affects the interpretation of cost breakdown structures. In the above example, it can be seen that there are some synergies between the intervention and the research question that justify a prescriptive stance in the empirical setting.

We would like to stress that interventionist studies positioned in the field of management accounting can relate to organisational change processes in many ways. From this perspective, the relationship between the key concepts—*management accounting, intervention and change*—can be quite multi-faceted. Figure 10.2 depicts a few possible relations between these issues.

The target of intervention can sometimes be directly related to (the process of) management accounting, which can be further seen as a part of organisation's present state (situation A). The idea behind the intervention could either be to preserve the present state or to launch a change process that is of interest *per se*. Another option is that the intervention focuses on some features of the organisation's current state other than management accounting, but it will nevertheless trigger a change process that will provide interesting research perspectives. Furthermore, it is possible that this change process has some reflections on the process of management accounting, which may be interesting from the research point of view.

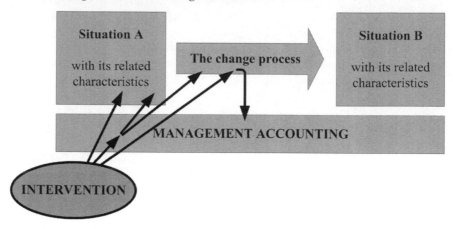

Figure 10.2   The target or focus of intervention.

"IV research has potential to provide researchers with a means to creating a real and direct impact outside the academic world (impact on society)"

"IV research should not only be seen as an approach for collecting empirical data but also as a vehicle for creating sustainable relations between academia and different industries"

Although this is not a methodological question, we feel that it is essentially important for a researcher in management accounting to be connected to the world of MA applications. Research, in this respect, is not an isolated island of thoughts but it is rather—we apologise for the clumsy metaphor—a vessel that commutes between the island and the mainland. Interventionist research is a valuable tool, though not the only one, in bridging the worlds of academic and practical interests. Our experience shows that managers are willing to participate in research projects where the actual intervention is of value to them. At the same time, while the value of intervention may sometimes be secondary for the researcher, engagement in the project may nevertheless open a lot of opportunities for academically interesting inquiries.

"The idea of the intervening researcher can be utilised in getting true (*emic*) access and acceptance within the host organisation."

An extreme case of this kind is the study on component commonality discussed in Chapter 4. During this process, which lasted for several years, the researcher reached the level of being 'one of us'. The roles and responsibilities of the researcher corresponded to those of an employee. This provided a good position for facilitating the change in question, a substantial one given the culture and traditions of the host organisation. Managers interviewed in our study pointed out quite clearly that it would be unlikely for a researcher to reach such a true *emic* position without the value proposition being connected to the process of interventions. This seems to be the case especially with relatively young researchers without significant 'brand value'.

> "Interventionist work may be one of the rare available research tools for studying issues that are 'bubbling under': issues that have not yet been extensively adopted by real life organisations."

Overall in the field of management accounting it is quite likely that situations will be identified where there is, first of all, a need to develop more advanced accounting tools or culture, such as long term cost modelling (a possible intervention). Only after that is it possible to assess the impact of these improved practices on the decision making process of the organisation (a possible research question, which resembles the situation in our study on life cycle costing discussed in Chapter 8). Interventionist management accounting research may thus be an effective way to investigate phenomena that are either new or difficult to find without needing to 'lurk' on the off-chance of finding an early adoptor or otherwise exceptional organisation. From this perspective, one of the strengths of the interventionist approach lies in its ability to provide effective access to an organisation and to facilitate the creation of a research setting with novelty value.

> "IV research can be regarded as a specific tool in a 'methodological toolbox' that should be fitted into a researcher's capabilities and into the possibilities occurring during a research topic's life cycle."

When focusing on one research approach, there is a clear risk of conveying a picture that this particular approach 'saves the world'. Without much need for elaboration, we acknowledge that interventionist research should be seen as a tool in a toolbox rather than a dominant world-view on management accounting research. We expect that MA would benefit from rich pluralism in research approaches.

> "IV research can be used as a mechanism for opening black boxes of organisational activities and, when applied with sufficient rigor, as a means of avoiding the problems connected with failing to recollect and/ or hiding undesired behaviour."

Emic-level hands-on approaches to data gathering are powerful tools for breaking into theoretical black boxes and for entering into discussions that are perceived as relevant by real-life organisations (illustrated in Chapter 6). For instance, in the project focusing on product costing development, the researchers' involvement in presenting product level cost data revealed the employee-level practices in applying and interpreting cost information. This was an observation which led to refinement of the original research question so that the decision-making context in the organisation was taken into account. In a similar vein, the project with an emphasis on service R&D (Chapter 5) travelled quite far from the original objective as it was noticed in the field that perceptions of the notion of service(s) varied substantially between individuals.

> "The act of intervention can be used for validating results immediately during the process of research. This supports both the relevance and efficiency of theory production."

Interventionist research, as we see it, poses quite naturally a good test of relevance. As Labro and Tuomela (2003) point out, the act of implementation is a central one in gaining understanding concerning the functioning or non-functioning of an idea. Intervention is typically about implementing something: a process model, a measure, a measurement system, or perhaps a novel engineering solution. During the process of implementation, as was the case in quality costing development (Chapter 8), it is necessary to question the fundamental premises related to the construct being implemented. This leads to findings and contributions which are at least locally tested and thus applicable.

For the sake of objectivity, it should be stressed that interventionist management accounting research does not only contain a lot of potential; there are also inherent risks and challenges associated with the approach. The main risks—as can be concluded on the basis of our experience—are discussed next.

RISKS IN INTERVENTIONIST MA RESEARCH

Our examples clearly show that interventionist research needs time. It needs a lot of time: the extensive length of the research processes without any certainty on an explicit academic outcome (publication) is a clear risk. In our experience, a typical interventionist project may last between two and six years, and it is likely that the first publications will only come out of the later phases of the venture.

Theoretical contributions do not always stem from individual projects but rather from a series of them. It might well be that the theoretical value is the final outcome of following a path that traces several individual projects and lucky coincidences and leads the researcher through different facets of the empirical world. As visibility of the theoretical value of empirical material is limited prior to the actual interventionist project, it is also possible that some interventions do not result in theoretical contributions but perhaps only in some practical insights. In that sense, it is truly about opening black boxes: it is ultimately only through the exposure of the 'content of the box' that the contribution potential can be evaluated. Unfortunately, in interventionist research this process may take several months or years.

On the other hand, it is rather unfair to characterise the existence of contribution potential as a dichotomy: contribution potential or not contribution potential. Perhaps contribution potential is not an absolute quality of a research setting, but is an issue that can be influenced by decisions during an interventionist project. Therefore it is critical that the researchers should be constantly alert to the possible theoretical connections of the observed events and phenomena. Without this alertness or awareness, the possible theoretical underpinnings are likely to go unnoticed and the opportunity for redirecting the research project is left unused.

Interventionist research plays with different interests and always involves at least two groups of stakeholder: those who intervene (researchers) and those which are being intervened into (companies, representatives of companies). A combination of strong managers and weak researchers is a vulnerable one. This means that researchers have to be able to recognise their own objectives and work towards them. Otherwise the outcome may be an unbalanced emphasis on practically relevant issues at the expense of academically interesting results. Managers are sometimes very skilful in guiding projects in directions that primarily achieve the expected value that they seek. It is in the researcher's interest to keep the manager happy and make sure that some sort of theoretical contribution will also follow. This is not an easy task.

Carrying out good interventionist research calls for many qualities and abilities. As a prerequisite, success in getting true 'emic' access, according to our experience, requires an ability to naturally interact with the managers (and with people at different levels of the organisation): using their language, and understanding their values and stances on different issues. At the same time, deriving academically acceptable output from the process—in other words, exploiting the access—requires good analytical skills, a versatile and to some extent multi-disciplinary knowledge-base, and methodological capabilities that facilitate handling both quantitative and qualitative data. It might be that the ideal combination of these abilities is very rarely to be achieved by a single individual. However, the diversity of pursued abilities may also be seen as a rationale for team-based interventionist research. It is much more realistic for a team to be able to combine and include all the necessary virtues than it is for an individual. Based on our experience, interventionist research is especially fruitful when it involves more than just one individual. Even if most of the empirical work is done by one person, the reflection phase benefits from the ideas of a wider community.

As Jönsson and Lukka (2007) phrased it, interventionist research can be seen as 'an experiment in the field'. It is about creating a real-life laboratory, within which something interesting can be tested. This raises not only ethical but also ontological and epistemological issues. In the case of strong interventions, there is a risk of creating highly idiosyncratic or even unrealistic settings ('synthetic anomalies'), which would not have been encountered without interventions. An example could be implementation of a management accounting technology in a very unlikely environment. Although this might be rare—given the two parties who are always included—the risk should be acknowledged that a strong individual researcher might be able to contribute to a state of affairs which could be seen as unnatural anywhere other than in that particular setting: the researcher is not facilitating a change but rather manipulating one. As a result, the suggested implications would only contain anecdotal value.

11 Managerial Perspectives
Interview Study

Thus far, this book has focused on *ex-post* analysis of selected research projects with interventionist elements in them. However, in addition to the *ex-post* analysis of conducted research projects, this book also provides empirical evidence on managers' perspectives on interventionist research and its potential in ensuring pragmatic relevance of the research results. In order to bring out the view of practitioners involved in these selected research projects, the most important industry participants were interviewed in order to reflect the process of interventionist research from their point of view.

NEED TO BRING MANAGERS AND SCHOLARS CLOSER TO EACH OTHER

Many practitioners and scholars have been concerned about the relevance of management accounting research. However, there are at least two approaches to this problem. On one hand, maybe the academic community has not been seeking enough opportunities to engage in collaboration with practitioners in order to find areas of research with shared interest. On the other hand, it is equally easy to say that maybe the industry has not been that active in seeking ways to collaborate with the academic community either. Nevertheless, interventionist research has been pointed out as one way to bring practitioners and researchers closer to each other and, hence, increase the pragmatic relevance of management accounting research. By engaging in interventionist research projects, companies will have access to knowledgeable resources while the researchers will gain access to interesting real-life settings which they can use to produce interesting academic contributions. In such arrangements, however, it is important to define the collaboration in a way that provides interesting results for both parties. If only practical results are highlighted, researchers might feel that they have not been able achieve their goals. However, if the projects only provide interesting academic results, the managers might feel that they have been taken advantage of. Hence, it is important to ensure that the interventionist research projects fulfil the objectives of both participating parties.

Part II provided examples of research interventions that the researchers of CMC have carried out in order to familiarise themselves with the case contexts and the practical phenomenon that they are studying—while still providing valuable contributions to the case companies. Sometimes research interventions have been rather narrow and focused on a pre-defined area within the case company. However, usually the research interventions have lasted several years and resulted in very close collaboration between the researchers and the participating managers. As the research collaboration advances and trust among the participants increases, researchers can actually become very important partners for managers and they start to talk about problems they might not wish to talk about even internally, let alone discuss with outsiders. Such relationships eventually tend to open up very interesting areas for research. In such projects, based on the experience of CMC, both managers and researchers are deeply committed to common goals and this sort of collaboration can result in very interesting results for both parties, hence bringing practitioners and researchers closer to each other.

One important aspect of this book was the analysis of the different types of research intervention done in the projects of CMC. For practitioners, this might give examples of industry–university collaboration such as most managers have never considered. Furthermore, in addition to the description and analysis of the interventions, this study also included interviews of managers who had participated in research projects with CMC in order to provide the practitioner's perspective on interventionist research. Four senior managers deeply involved in the long-term research collaboration were interviewed:

- Managing Director (case discussed in Chapter 4)
- Financial Director (Chapter 6)
- Global Product Line Manager (Chapters 5 and 7)
- Vice President, Quality and Development (Chapter 8)

The semi-structured, qualitative interviews lasted about two hours per manager. All these managers have not only been important spokespeople for the research collaboration inside their own organisations but have also participated actively in different research efforts. Because of the long-term research collaboration, the researchers and the managers knew each other and the discussion of both the advantages and disadvantages seemed very open. During the interviews, the managers pointed out a few very interesting aspects that have not yet been explicitly discussed in the literature on interventionist management accounting research.

IMPORTANCE OF PRACTICAL OBJECTIVES

One reason why the practitioners' point of view has not been that widely discussed could be that the existing literature focuses more on the research perspective and, therefore, the practitioners' point of view simply has not been considered that relevant. However, when considering access to the case companies, all the managers pointed out that these research projects need to provide them with concrete benefits, otherwise they have no reason to engage in such projects:

> *Before I can commit myself to a project, I need to be sure that the concept has potential.*

At the beginning of the project, these managers need to commit themselves to providing lots of information to the researchers and, if they are not certain about the potential benefits, they simply cannot allocate the time and other resources. The managerial perspective on research simply might not have been that relevant for researchers whose challenge was primarily to convince research funders rather than managers. However, when engaged in the interventionist research, finding companies and managers willing to interact with scholars is rather different from convincing research funders.

It was also very eye-opening to discover that the managers do not see these projects as research projects. On the contrary, they seemed to have their own objectives for the collaboration:

> *We do not see these primarily as research projects but rather as development projects. However, when thinking about it, development projects usually have a clearly defined goal and milestones whereas the research projects have been seen more as explorations—you never really know what you will find.*

One manager also pointed out the need to combine these elements and that it also is somehow related to the life cycle of the research project:

> *Such a research project has two components. On one hand, it is very long-term oriented and it is difficult to see the results. On the other hand, these projects tend to also have the more pragmatic element in them. It seems that this role changes over time. Usually, the more analytical phase is at the beginning and it is difficult to point out exactly what the outcome will be. However, once the situation has been analysed thoroughly, the project enters the development stage when the results also become more concrete. Sometimes at the beginning I have felt that this is not going anywhere but, if the homework has been done properly, new and interesting results keep popping up all the time!*

Even though all the managers pointed out that these projects are primarily seen as development projects and not as research projects, they saw the fact that they were also research projects positively so long as good development projects benefited the career of the researchers in the form of interesting publications. It was also considered important that the objectives for research interventions are set in collaboration. Some managers even had experience in research where the primary focus had been on scientific publications:

> *It was important that goals were set together and both parties were sparring with each other. The results gave the direction for the next steps and not just one academic publication. We have some research partners from universities in technical development and sometimes I get the feeling that they are working only for their publications . . .*

It is also interesting to note that, in many cases, the results achieved in one project have set the ground for the next one. This seems to be an important element when considering the life cycle of research collaboration.

INTERVENTIONIST RESEARCH REQUIRES ACCESS TO REAL DATA

In order for the interventionist research projects to be successful, companies need to commit their own resources to these projects as well. No matter how active the researchers are, if the managers do not invest their time in the projects, it will be a panacea. Furthermore, companies need to provide access to data. However, in management accounting areas, this can easily become a problem. Companies seem reluctant to provide access to researchers because they consider financial information to be very crucial information, for some reason. However, as pointed out by one of the interviewees, in most companies lots of data in ERP systems are useless anyway, so why should they be so jealous about it?

> *In many cases [the access to real cost information] is considered a very sensitive issue but no-one inside the company can make any sense out of it anyway. Thus, why not let somebody else try? If someone then wants to misuse that information, they need to have access to so many other things that the misuse of that information is not really that realistic.*

Thus, as pointed out in the comment above, even some product cost analyses are useless unless the reader has access to all the details of the costing model in order to form an understanding as to how these analyses have been provided. In other words, managers tend to overstate the risks in letting researchers become involved in cost management projects with them.

NEED TO FIND SUITABLE PARTNER ORGANISATIONS
AND PARTNERS IN ORGANISATIONS

The managers also pointed out that it is important to find individuals and companies that are willing to develop their competences—otherwise the company is not going to be able to provide the support that interventionist researchers need in order to gain good results. The managers need to have the willingness to develop their understanding and also the willingness to question their own ways of thinking:

> *It was important to have other companies involved in the research projects so we could discuss with researchers and also managers of other companies. It was also important that we were able to laugh at our own mistakes. It really has been fun to analyse our actions in a positive ways and learn from our own mistakes.*

The researchers can also be seen as neutral partners who can be used to enhance communication between companies and departments inside one company. Thus, it is important to find managers who are willing to challenge managers from different functions in positive ways, and to invite them into dialogue with each other. Finally, especially in financial departments, there may be no such development positions existing in product and business development areas. Hence, management accounting researchers can actually provide valuable resources for managers and in that way interventionist research might actually turn out to be very beneficial method of collaboration.

MANAGERS NEED PATIENCE—
RESEARCHERS ARE NOT CONSULTANTS

The interviewees also pointed out that interventionist research seems to need quite long research projects because it takes time to build trust and commitment among the different participants. Managers often expect results too quickly even if one important stage in research projects is the understanding of the big picture and the context. In other words, in many cases the start of the projects might have seemed a bit slow when the researchers have been working with the managers in order to find the right problems, but if that phase is done properly, the final outcomes of the research collaboration might turn out to be extraordinary.

The managers pointed out that this deep commitment to understanding the context is the main difference between interventionist research and consulting:

> *It is typical that the researchers have been digging up information and studying all the dirty details. Lots of data have been gathered from different sources, manually fed into large Excel sheets or Access databases and, finally, analysed. This is really something that is impossible to do with consultants. Researchers are motivated and willing to dig up information and find the answers, which is exactly what is needed. Consultants do not want to get their hands dirty even though the solutions are not found in upper-level discussions and PowerPoint presentations.*

> *There are different situations that suit using a consultant or a researcher. At the strategy level, consultants are more efficient. They have lots of benchmark information from other organisations and that is what they mostly provide for us. If there is a certain problem inside our organisation that needs detailed attention, researchers are much better because they are willing to dig deeper.*

Based on these comments, it is interesting that the critics of interventionist research focus so much on linking research interventions with consulting. The worry should rather be on what is the difference between working for the organisation and the research interventions. As pointed out by the managing director of the case company discussed in Chapter 4:

> *The ways of doing things between researchers and consultants is very different, the researcher is more like one of our employees. Consultants have their slideshows and answers before they even know the problem. I prefer the approach that we work together to find out the real problem and then start looking for the solution.*

This discussion on linking interventionist research with consulting could be further elaborated with the comment of the Managing Director cited above:

> *Consultants have also realised that, in order to remain competitive, they have to go into this direction as well . . .*

Therefore, to rattle the cage, the question should not be whether the interventionist research is close to consulting but rather whether consulting is evolving in the direction of interventionist research. This, however, is rather dependent on what is seen as a research intervention.

Despite the fact that the interviewees appreciated the long-term commitment of the researchers, they also pointed out that some preliminary results are needed quickly in order to commit other managers and company employees to the projects. Thus, the projects should be designed in a way that some interesting results can be found quite quickly before, perhaps, entering into more deep analysis. For example, the preliminary results could be hard facts on certain problematic issues which then would motivate the managers to commit their time and efforts in order to analyse the situation further and, eventually, come up with a good plan to solve the problems.

HOW TO BECOME 'ONE OF US'?

As was pointed out, managers of the case companies do not compare intervening researchers with consultants but rather with their own employees.

Thus the researchers, in many cases, have been able to become 'one of us'. In other words, the researchers have become insiders and hence have reached the *emic* level. However, it is not self-evident that the 'one of us' status will be reached, as was pointed out by one of the interviewees:

> *Getting real access and acceptance inside the organisation is rather challenging. It is like in sales, you first have to sell yourself as a person. It requires quite a lot of social skills because, in many cases, the researcher is considered as a threat by many people inside the organisation. People do not understand why some young guys come and start asking questions. The employees feel that they know these things already since they have been doing things for a long time already.*
>
> *The researchers need to be able to ask things in a way that does not irritate the employees and managers too much. It is really challenging for an outsider to create the status of an insider and the only way to do this is to be present and work together with the people inside the organisation. If the young researcher had been bossing around and made the design engineers do the drawings instead of learning to use our CAD system himself, the organisation might have had a somewhat different attitude towards him.*

One interviewee also pointed out that the organisation is most likely to accept the researcher as 'one of us' when they see the first results. That is also one reason why the importance of the first results cannot be emphasised too much.

> *The first results! Only after the first results is it possible to ensure that the damn fellow is right. That is how you break the organisational resistance. However, it is also important to communicate the results in a way that this was done together!*

Thus, in order to get the *emic* role, when both the first and the final results are presented the credit for the results must be shared with the employees as well. When the employees and managers are given some credit for the results of the research projects, it will motivate them to engage in other interventionist research projects in the future as well.

Finally, it was also explicitly pointed out that, in order to reach the *emic* level, a relatively long time frame is needed:

> *Definitely this process needs time, one year is not enough for that [reaching the status as 'one of us'].*

To summarise, interventionist research provides interesting opportunities both for researchers and practitioners. In many cases, practitioners are interested in many new things but they do not have the time to commit to implementing the most recent management accounting innovations. However, by engaging in interventionist research projects with universities, the researchers might provide at least some of the resources needed for the implementation process. At the same time, the researchers would have a chance to learn from those interesting new management accounting innovations and their functionality in real-life settings. In a sense, instead of searching for a company that has already implemented these new tools or management concepts, researchers can actually choose another strategy by creating the setting in which to study that particular phenomenon. Participation in the implementation process also provides the researchers with a deep practical understanding of the phenomenon. Thus, interventionist research, at best, provides a very interesting win-win situation for both practitioners and researchers.

12 Towards a Typology of Research Interventions

One of the aims of this book was to sketch a preliminary typology or classification for interventionist studies. Based on the tool developed for our *ex-post* analysis, we suggest considering three dimensions for structuring the domain of IV research in MA:

- Strength of intervention (Jönsson and Lukka 2007)
  - From modest to strong
- Paradigmatic frame (cf. Ahrens and Chapman 2006; Kakkuri-Knuuttila et al. 2008)
  - Objective vs. subjective
- Management accounting focus in the actual intervention
  - From inside MA to non-MA

FOUR ARCHETYPES OF INTERVENTIONIST RESEARCH

By relying on the first two dimensions, we can derive four possible archetypes of interventionist studies, each having a distinct character. As the number of conducted interventionist studies is very limited to date, we do not try to classify the existing ones into the suggested types but rather try to evoke a discussion of the types and their features at the general level. Let us now look at these four archetypes in more detail.

First, studies with modest interventions and a subjective paradigmatic frame are likely to be applicable for investigating phenomena that are reasonably well-known (established) in practice, but that lack elaborated theoretical underpinnings and sense-making. It is acknowledged that modest interventions may also take place in many studies that are not necessarily labelled as interventionist. Long-lasting observatory presence in an empirical setting may leave footprints that equate to intentional interventions. Thus from a distance, studies with modest interventions and a subjective stance largely resemble traditional and usually extensive case studies that investigate contemporary phenomena in a real-life setting and that explicitly address the individuals' subjective interpretations of the meanings of witnessed events. These are studies which do not always explicitly underscore the role of researchers' interventions or active involvement (see, e.g., Flyvbjerg 2006, Gummesson 1993). However, in contrast with case studies focusing on subjective meanings, interventionist studies (even in a modest form) wittingly employ interventions as research tools, as described, in creating an interesting setting or in securing a promising access.

Secondly, let us look at studies classified as modest and objective. Before going any further towards a clear-cut subjective/objective classification, we wish to point out that we largely share the spirit of Ahrens (2008) in that:

> *We cannot look into people's hearts and minds and we also cannot comprehensively capture the complexity of social reality. Instead of guessing subjective meanings or trying to find quantitative proxies for social reality, interpretive management accounting researchers have found ways of studying how understandings of accounting play out in diverse activities which may engage with, or distance themselves from, social discourses, practices, material arrangements, and structures of intentionality.*

In a similar vein, we can identify a domain of case studies which in general is oriented towards more objective connotations of objective reality, although some subjective elements may be included as well (cf. Yin 1994, Eisenhardt 1989). In interventionist management accounting research, subjective and objective (*emic*, *etic*) emphasis may vary during the life cycle of a study as suggested by Jönsson and Lukka (2005). In other words, we would be unlikely to find purely objective interventionist studies, but studies with more emphasis on an *etic*/objective perspective could well be encountered. This would be the case especially when a multiple-case approach was to be adopted in interventionist research.

Let us move now to the world of strong interventions. The third archetype would consist of studies classified as strong and subjective. Strong interventions could be recommended, for instance, when the question of interest requires substantial improvements in relation to the present state of an organisation. As suggested earlier, novel management accounting approaches may not be easily found as readily implemented. This may call for an interventionist approach, a kind of field experiment, where a setting has to be built first. When practised in subjective variations, studies with strong interventions provide multi-dimensional, and sometimes surprising, possibilities for analysis and reflection. Also, strong and subjective studies require a lot from the company–researcher collaboration: accomplishing strong mutual interventions means substantial investments in actual development work, but at the same time, subjective reflection by the researcher may not be easily translated into something the company greatly appreciates.

Finally, we may also identify strong and objective studies; in other words, studies that benefit from an *emic* viewpoint when making interventions but that concentrate more on an *etic* level when conducting analysis and reflection. The study by Lyly-Yrjänäinen (2008) on component commonality and its cost management implications, which is partly discussed in Chapter 4, fulfils the criteria of this type. Management accounting and cost management in relation to commonality were not approached from the viewpoint of subjective meanings and rationales but rather from the perspective of more general frameworks and measurement principles that could be applied within the described circumstances, given the factual logic of cost behaviour.

As we see it, and in contrast to some degree with crossing the borders between the four presented archetypes, the combination of these four with a management accounting focus (the third dimension) should not be regarded as a crucial thing at the level of *research design*. This is not to say that the designs of individual studies—being interventionist or non-interventionist—would not be partly affected by the subjects of interest, but nevertheless, similar designs may still be applied despite the variety in substance. The question of MA focus in actual intervention has an impact predominantly on the set of skills and capabilities required of the researcher: carrying out interventionist MA research with non-accounting interventions may call for inter-disciplinary research teams in order to secure the necessary versatility of expertise.

FOCAL POINT OF RESEARCH INTERVENTIONS

Given the tradition in empirical management accounting research of focusing on (and trying to contribute to) more the practice of *management accounting* (cf. Malmi and Granlund 2009) rather than organisational practices *in general*[1], we feel it is a point worth making that valuable management accounting contributions can also be made by entering into the empirical realms of other disciplines. To make this point a bit clearer, consider the following citation (Inaga and Schneider 2005, p. 239):

> *The many breakthroughs today in medical practice would have been impossible without medical research. In medicine, there is a symbiotic relationship among medical research, medical education, and medical practice. The picture is different in accounting. The relationship is disjointed, with wide gaps between accounting education, accounting research, and accounting practice.*

Indeed, the synergies between accounting research and practice do seem to resemble those between medical research and practice. However, there is a clear distinction: those who practise medicine are trained doctors whereas those who practise (management) accounting do not have to be trained nor do they have to be well-focused experts. In fact, they might be engineers who are thrilled by technical aspects, or they might be leaders driven by an interest in human behaviour. Management accounting is a playground that includes a variety of people with a variety of backgrounds and a number of agendas. Thus, depending on the empirical situation, the organisational change process that evokes interesting outlooks for a management accounting researcher can be facilitated by a catalyst using a set of different methods. Some of them might be more directly related to management accounting whereas other may not have that quality. However the change process, when taking place inside an organisation, always contains accounting-related connotations. This offers good prospects for MA scholars to immigrate into real-life organisations.

SUMMARISING THE ANALYSIS OF RESEARCH PROJECTS

The suggested classification of interventionist research based on three dimensions should be seen as tentative. There is a variety of other variables that might be used in classifying the variations of interventionist work. Table 12.1 depicts a more refined analysis of conducted projects based on a number of variables (units of analysis), including (1) the motivation for access, (2) the time line of the project, (3) the process for specifying the research question, (4) intervention focus, (5) strength of identified interventions, (6) the practical contribution and (7) the theoretical contribution. As we see it, the analysis presented in Table 12.1 serves as a template for further discussions on the varying nature of interventionist management accounting research.

As shown by our analysis, there is good scope for different types of intervention in management accounting research and, as a result, different perspectives for analysing these interventions as well. A perspective already identified in the literature (Jönsson and Lukka 2005) is the strength of the research intervention. In some cases, the research intervention can be rather shallow while in other cases the researchers might engage in very long, intensive and effective collaboration with the case company. Another important perspective deals with the purpose of—or logic behind—the intervention. Research interventions can either directly focus on the issues that are academically interesting or on providing a setting within which to analyse something that is academically interesting. Sometimes interventions can even be carried out only to gain access to a company of interest in order to study something which remains rather ambiguous during the initial phases.

In the examples discussed here, research interventions were sometimes defined in advance to fit in with the scientific objectives (expected contribution) whereas, in other cases, the connections between the actual contribution and the intervention were less engineered. In addition, it is possible to take an even more radical approach to the interventionist participation. When the researchers become active participants in organisational development processes, the collaboration with the managers and the evolving trust between them might encourage the managers to bring up issues they would never reveal to an 'outsider' and, hence, totally unexpected and interesting topics for research might be opened up. This is precisely the advantage of the interventionist research approach. In fact, most CMC projects start with analysing product and customer profitability which, as such, do not possess novelty value. However, as these projects advance, more interesting questions are likely to surface and these questions often provide potential for theoretical contribution, while at the same time they cover issues that are of widespread managerial interest. Furthermore, when the initial interventions have quite pragmatic objectives, managers are more likely to commit themselves to the research collaboration because it will provide some value to them. It is still a challenge to convince managers about the benefits that interventionist research projects can provide to them.

AREAS OF FURTHER RESEARCH IN TERMS OF INTERVENTIONIST MA RESEARCH

In all, our book suggests several interesting topics for further research. First, the tentative classification scheme presented above deserves more empirical testing within different cultural contexts. It is likely that these tests would be able to further refine and elaborate the suggested template. Secondly, if the interventionist research approach attempts to increase managerial interest in research collaboration, it might be justified to ask the managers more systematically what sort of research they would be interested in and how they would prefer to work with the researchers.

The interviews conveyed that interventionist research certainly has potential but that it requires both good skills and the right attitude in the researcher—as well as explicit discussions on managerial interests connected with the study. Detailed elaboration of these issues might be a possibility for further research as well.

We also feel that sense-making of the interventionist research *process* is far from complete. Based on the interviews, it seems that managers—even within one company—might have rather different perceptions of the process they personally have been engaged in. However, managers have found the researcher-practitioner team a powerful combination when solving organisational problems. Furthermore, when exposed to the challenges of real-life managerial decision making, the researchers also have an opportunity to get new and relevant insights into many academic issues. Thus this motivates one to further address the value of the academic–practitioner team in interventionist management accounting research.

Table 12.1   Analysis of the Selected Research Projects

Analyzed interventionist research projects or streams	The units of analysis		
	The motivation of access	*Timeline*	*Research question specification process*
Component commonality and its cost implications (Chapter 4)	Expert role and available external resource. Good personal relationships. Initially a need for improved activity-level costing; later the challenge of modular product architecture, which was partly inspired by an experience from another company working with CMC.	First project started in 2000, second project in another setting in 2003. The main part of the research activities have been conducted by the end of 2007.	The process lasted several years. The final research question was formulated in the later stages of the project. It can be argued that the final question was influenced by the reflection-phase of the process.
Service R&D and its MA implications (Chapter 5)	The long history of collaboration between CMC and the organization. The unofficial but effective role of CMC as a partner that is partly responsible for the development of management accounting in the organization.	Two formal projects that were much connected with each other. First project 2003–2005. Second project 2006–2008.	The initial research question was a result of long-lasting collaboration prior to the interventionist study. However, the initial question was translated to more broad conceptual and paradigmatic questions during the project. In other words, it was initially expected that the study would be tightly in connection with MA, but this link proved to be more indirect.

The units of analysis			
Focus of intervention	*Strength of intervention*	*Practical contribution*	*Theoretical contribution*
In the beginning, there were interventions focusing on management accounting; however, the main focus and emphasis through the process has been on engineering and product development. Interventions in this technical area have been supported by management accounting interventions.	Increasingly strong. At the beginning, more external expert role but gradually status as a full member of the organization: possibility to observe a variety of corporate routines and paradigms.	Technical product architecture -related solutions that have shown their potential in the business of client organization. Improved understanding about the cost behaviour of component commonality.	Moving the commonality discussion (especially cost effects of commonality) from make-to-stock (MTS) and assembly-to-order (ATO) to engineering-to-order (ETO) context. In other words, broadening the scope of extant component commonality theory. In short, the research stream's contribution lies first in its ability to explicate the implications of context in component commonality and second, in its insight into management accounting related to component commonality.
Interventions were about supporting the service R&D of the focal company through different analyses and participation on development activities. During the project, the researchers analyzed the key service technologies available in the company in order to proceed in the research project. In a meeting, for instance, a process specialist asked for advice in the further development of the cost accounting part of a simulation tool on the customers' business, used to support consultancy.	Strong interventions were made during the project. The role of the researchers was very close to the employees of the organization.	The main source of practical contribution from the research project is the business game concept developed with the help of CMC representatives. In addition to the game concept as such, some findings during the R&D project may be of importance for the company. It is expected that the findings on the nature of service R&D projects facilitate the R&D management developments in the company.	The project represents a learning process focusing on the characteristics of service, especially in one business context. Referring to the existing management accounting literature, it is unusual that the real-life decision-making situations and the accounting objects can be analyzed in such a detailed manner and based on a longitudinal data, such as in this study. The study is an attempt to respond the request in the contingency-based accounting literature, for functional level and project-level analyses of control systems.

(*continued*)

Table 12.1   Analysis of the Selected Research Projects

Analyzed interventionist research projects or streams	The units of analysis		
	The motivation of access	Timeline	Research question specification process
Product cost information for decision making (Chapter 6)	Available external resource for improving the current situation characterized by the lack of product-level cost-consciousness; further access through following the questions that had been raised on the basis of initial work.	Three formally separate but thematically connected projects. First between years 1999–2000, second 2001–2003 and third 2005–2006.	Projects were based on relatively clear agenda. However this agenda was not primarily based on the identification of interesting research questions; rather, it was expected that practical cost management development work would provide a number of potential contributions. Research question formulation by following the questions raised by the company after interventions.
Cost management in business networks (Chapter 7)	Available external resources and relevant expertise. Good personal-level connections between organizations.	Two separate projects in two different supply networks. First interventionist project 1999–2001, second 2003–2005.	The final research question has been found as late as in the reflection phase; however, the practical questions in mind when starting the project were not far from the final question. The main difference being that initially it was expected that descriptions on OBA would be sufficient for MA contribution.

The units of analysis			
Focus of intervention	*Strength of intervention*	*Practical contribution*	*Theoretical contribution*
Management accounting and product costing: developing applications and systems enabling the production of cost information for product decisions and profitability management. In the later stages, some of the interventions were focused on supply chain development by facilitating communication between the focal company and its suppliers.	Can be characterized as semi-strong. Interventions were stronger and more concrete than taking part on discussions but researchers kept some distance on actual decision-making and were not true citizens of the organization.	The projects have resulted in a number of actions taken by the organization, for instance: Adjusting the pricing of products and spare part items, supply chain re-organization, increased attention to end-of-life decisions Overall, the projects have resulted in increase in the level of cost-consciousness.	The projects have produced contribution on the practice of activity-based costing in manufacturing setting (partly confirming and refining extant findings). More specifically, interventionist work has produced insight into more general causes and effects of profitability. In addition, part of the contribution lies in the analysis of after sales profitability and its connection to product-level profitability.
The focus was on the costing development for open-book accounting in supplier companies. Also the role of the researches involved acting as a neutral part in the actual open-book negotiations between suppliers and a customer. Interventions in costing development were strong and they lead to explicit implications.	In network setting, the researchers did not necessarily reach a true emic perspective in any of the organizations but nevertheless had a valuable position in observing network cost management practices.	In short, the interventions enabled the OBA exercises in the two networks. In that sense, the practical contribution was a clear and measurable one.	The theoretical contribution of this stream lies in exposing "the different faces" of open-book accounting. The research enabled, based on exceptionally detailed data on real-life open-book accounting, an analysis that contributes to the positioning of open-book accounting in the management control variants or archetypes.

(continued)

Table 12.1 Analysis of the Selected Research Projects

Analyzed interventionist research projects or streams	The units of analysis		
	The motivation of access	*Timeline*	*Research question specification process*
Measuring cost efficiency (Chapter 8)	The history of collaboration between the organization and CMC. Also a good match between the expected required expertise and the external supply of resources.	The first steps of collaboration in another topic area in 2001–2005. Interventionist projects during the years 2006–2008.	The first set of research questions were formulated rapidly in the beginning of the process jointly with company representatives. The second set of research questions emerged during the first part of the project. The reflection phases of the research stream produced yet another domain of questions that could be partly answered through the empirical data gathered.
Life cycle costing (Chapter 9)	Sequential: 1) initial recognition of organization's need to improve the cost accounting of its fixed assets 2) formulation of project by researchers that would respond to this need 3) Finding the actual and specific way of collaboration around issue. Also influenced by the history of CMC with empirical work in the subject area.	Roots in early 2000. Later, a couple of projects gathering empirical data through interviews and surveys in 2003. Interventionist work during the years 2004–2007.	Interventionist work was started with a rather clearly formulated research question; however, this formulation was made without in-depth understanding of the focal organization. As a result, the second interventionist project was established with a question more based on the current state of the organization.

The units of analysis

Focus of intervention	Strength of intervention	Practical contribution	Theoretical contribution
The focus was mainly in the domain of management accounting or more broadly in performance measurement and management: measures for quality management and sourcing management were constructed. However, not only measures were developed but also current processes were critically evaluated and improvements were proposed and discussed	Interventions on measures/measurement development classified as strong: the role of the researchers was to establish and implement well-justified and expedient measures. As a result, the company's toolbox for the management of quality and sourcing was enhanced. During some parts of the process, the role of the researcher resembled that of an employee.	From the company's perspective, the research project was able provide answers to the initial questions. As a result, the researchers developed a model that is able to estimate the quality costs in the future (rolling forecast) at a given uncertainty. The model has been now empirically validated for almost two years, and the company has been active in utilizing it. Also purchasing management has adopted a number of principles developed in the project related especially on the total cost of ownership–issues.	As a part of theoretical contribution of the project, the concern about the validity of popular quality measures has been brought up. The context of quality cost measurement in project business, which draws on the experiences of the interventionist project, is used as an illustrative example of the challenges that might be faced while striving to maintain validity of performance measures. Essentially, the paper points out that some surrogate ratios (such as quality costs/sales) have become so established that their validity has not been seriously considered at the conceptual level. It is stressed that validity is always constructed into the measures used in a given context and threats to validity may be faced at any step from defining the concept and operationalizing the definition to actual measurement.
In the first intervention, the focus was comprehensively on management accounting applications; that is, an intervention was made in order to develop a feasible means to conduct life cycle cost analyses. However, the second set of interventions was more about sourcing practices and thus process development than management accounting.	The first set of interventions on management accounting was semi-strong with a clear and relatively narrow focus and objectives. However, the role of the researchers was to be external expert rather than true insider. The second set of interventions was more weak: discussion-based interaction with the representatives of the organisation	The research stream provided the organization with a more elaborated sourcing framework with a template for playing with the different criteria present in decision-making. In addition, a LCC model was constructed that facilitated life cycle costing with input information that is realistically available in the organization.	The main theoretical contribution is the explication of the dynamic role of life cycle costing; dynamic in a sense, that its applications and limitations are connected with the stage of life cycle. It was shown that practicing life cycle costing is an iterative process which will be rewarded by increasingly accurate long-term cost consciousness.

Notes

NOTE TO CHAPTER 2

1. Emphasis added. Indeed, whereas MA scholars either implicitly or explicitly regard interventionist studies in management accounting as studies with the researcher's activities focused in changing MA practices, we suggest a more flexible interpretation. In short, we argue that interventionist work does not have to deal with *MA change* only; it can also deal with a change *in which MA has a role* to play.

NOTE TO CHAPTER 12

1. By no means have we suggested that there is something wrong with this focus. But given the inter-disciplinary nature of management accounting, we should not leave this potential unused.

Bibliography

Ahrens, T., 2008. Overcoming the subjective-objective divide in interpretive management accounting research. *Accounting, Organizations and Society*, 33(2–3), pp. 292–297.

Ahrens, T. and Chapman, C., 2006. Doing qualitative field research in management accounting: Positioning data to contribute to theory. *Accounting, Organizations and Society*, 31(8), pp. 819–841.

Ahrens, T. and Chapman, C., 2007. Management accounting as practice. *Accounting, Organizations and Society*, 32(1–2), pp. 1–27.

Ahrens et al. 2008. The future of internpretive accounting research—A polyphonic debate. *Critical Perspectives on Accounting*, 19(6), pp. 867–879.

Agndal, H. and Nilsson, U., 2009. Interorganizational cost management in the exchange process. *Management Accounting Research*, 20(2), pp. 85–101.

Albright, T. L. and Roth, H., 1992. The measurement of quality costs: An alternative paradigm. *Accounting Horizons*, 6(2), pp. 15–27.

Amaro, G., Hendry, L and Kingsman, B., 1999. Competitive advantage, customisation and a new taxonomy for non make-to-stock companies. *International Journal of Operations & Production Management*, 19(4), pp. 349–371.

Anderson, S. W. and Sedatole, K., 1998. Designing quality into products: The use of accounting data in new product development. *Accounting Horizons*, 12(3), pp. 213–233.

Argyris, C., Putnam, R. and McLain Smith, D., 1985. *Action science*. San Francisco: Jossey-Bass.

Asiedu, Y. and Gu, P., 1998. Product life cycle cost analysis: state of the art review. *International journal of production research*, 36(4), pp. 883–908.

Bonoma, T. V., 1985. Case Research in Marketing: Opportunities, Problems, and a Process. *Journal of Marketing Research*, 22(2), pp. 199–208.

Booth, R., 1994. Life cycle costing. *Management Accounting*, 72(6).

Burchell, S., Clubb, C. and Hopwood, A., 1985. Towards a history of value added in the United Kingdom. *Accounting, Organizations and Society*, 10(4), pp. 381–413.

Burrell, G. and Morgan, G., 1979. *Sociological paradigms and organizational analysis: Elements of the sociology of corporate life*. London: Heinemann.

Carr, C. and Ng, J., 1995. Total cost control: Nissan and its U.K. supplier partnerships. *Management Accounting Research*, 6(4), pp. 347–365.

Chapman, C., 1997. Reflections on a contingent view of accounting. *Accounting, Organizations and Society*, 22(2), pp. 189–205.

Collier, D., 1981. The measurement and operating benefits of component part commonality. *Decision Science* 12(1), pp. 85–96.

Collier, D., 1982. Aggregate safety stock levels and component part commonality. *Decision Science* 28(11), pp. 1296–1303.

Cooper, R. and Slagmulder, R., 2004. Interorganizational cost management and relational context. *Accounting, Organizations and Society*, 29(1), pp. 1–26.

Crosby, P. B., 1979. *Quality is free.* New York: McGraw-Hill.

Day, R. L. and Herbig, P. A., 1990. How the Diffusion of Industrial Innovations is Different from New Retail Products. *Industrial Marketing Management,* 19(3), pp. 261–266.

Dekker, H. C., 2003. Value chain analysis in interfirm relationships: a field study. *Management Accounting Research*, 14(1), pp. 1–23.

Eisenhardt, K. M., 1989. Building Theories from Case Study Research. *Academy of Management Review*, 14(4), pp. 532–550.

Ellram, L., 1995. Total cost of ownership: an analysis approach for purchasing. *International journal of physical distribution & logistics management*, 25(8), pp. 4–23.

Eynan, A. and Rosenblatt, M. J., 1996. Component commonality effects on inventory costs. *IEE Transactions*, 28(2), pp. 93–104.

Feigenbaum, A. V., 1961. *Total quality control.* New York: McGraw-Hill.

Ferreira, L. D. and Merchant, K. A., 1992. Field Research in Management Accounting and Control: A Review and Evaluation. *Accounting, Auditing & Accountability Journal*, 5(4), pp. 3–34.

Flyvbjerg, B., 2006. Five misunderstandings about case study research. Qualitative Inquiry, 12(2), pp. 219–245.

Fong, D. K. H., Fu, H. and Li, Z., 2004. Efficiency in shortage reduction when using a more expensive common component. *Computers and Operations Research*, 31(1), pp. 123–138.

Gebauer, H., Fleisch, E. and Friedli, T., 2005. Overcoming the Service Paradox in Manufacturing Companies. *European Management Journal*, 23(1), pp. 14–26.

Gerchak, Y., Magazine, M. J. and Gamble, A. B., 1988. Component commonality with service level requirements. *Management Science* 34(6), pp. 753–760.

Gummesson, E., 1993. *Case study research in management: Method for generating qualitative data.* Stockholm University.

Grönroos, C., 2000. *Service Management and Marketing A Customer Relationship Management Approach.* Chichester: John Wiley & Sons Ltd.

Handfield, R. and Melnyk, S., 1998. The scientific theory-building process: a primer using the case of TQM. *Journal of Operations Management*, 16(4), pp. 321–339.

Hastrup, K., 1997. The dynamics of anthropological theory. *Cultural Dynamics*, 9(3), pp. 351–371.

Hicks, C. and Braiden, M., 2000. Computer aided production management issues in the engineering-to-order production of complex capital goods explored using a simulation approach. *International journal of production research*, 38(18), pp. 4783–4810.

Hicks, C., McGovern, T. and Earl, C., 2001. A typology of UK engineer to order companies. *International Journal of Logicstics: Research and Applications* 4(1), pp. 43–56.

Hillier, M., 2000. Component commonality in multiple-period, assemble-to-order systems. *IIE Transactions*, 32(8), pp. 755–766.

Hillier, M., 2002. Using commonality as backup safety stock. *European Journal of Operational Research*, 136(2), pp. 353–365.

Hopwood, A. G. (1983) On trying to study accounting in the context in which it operates. *Accounting, Organizations and society* 8(2/3), 287-305

Hopwood, A. G., 2002. If only there were simple solutions, but there aren't': some reflections on Zimmerman's critique of empirical management accounting research. *The European Accounting Review,* 11(4), pp. 777–785.

Håkansson, H. and Lind, J., 2004. Accounting and Network Coordination. *Accounting, Organizations and Society,* 29(1), pp. 51–72.

Ijiri, Y., 1975. *Theory of Accounting Measurement*. Sarasota: American Accounting Association.

Inanga, E. and Schneider, B., 2005. The failure of accounting research to improve accounting practice: a problem of theory and lack of communication. *Critical Perspectives on Accounting* 16(3), pp. 227–248.

Ittner, C. D., 1996. Exploratory Evidence on the Behavior of Quality Costs. *Operations Research*, 44(1), pp. 114–130.

Ittner, C. D. and Larcker, D. F., 2002. Empirical managerial accounting research: are we just describing management consulting practice? *The European Accounting Review*, 11(4), pp. 787–794.

Jackson, D.W. and Ostrom, L. L., 1980. Life Cycle Costing in Industrial Purchasing, *Journal of Purchasing and Materials Management*, 16(4), pp. 8–12.

Järvinen, A., 2004. *Elinkaarilaskennan nykytila*. Tampere University of Technology. (Master's Thesis).

Järvinen, A., Suomala, P. and Paranko, J., 2004. *Elinkaarilaskennan nykytila raideliikenteen toimitusketjussa*. Tampere: Tampere University of Technology.

Johansson, P. and Olhager, J., 2004. Industrial service profiling: Matching service offerings and processes. *International Journal of Production Economics*, 89(3), pp. 309–20.

Johnson, T. H. and Kaplan, R. S., 1987. *Relevance Lost: The Rise and Fall of Management Accounting*. Boston: Harvard Business School Press.

Jönsson, S. and Lukka K., 2005. *Doing interventionist research in management accounting*. GRI-rapport 2005:6. Gothenburg, Gothenburg Research Institute.

Jönsson, S. and Lukka, K., 2007. There and Back Again: Doing Interventionist Research in Management Accounting. In: C. Chapman, A. Hopwood, M. Shields, eds. *Handbook of Management Accounting Research, Volume 1*, Oxford: Elsevier, pp. 373–392.

Juran, J. M. and Gryna, F. M., 1993. *Quality planning and analysis*, 3rd Edition, New York: McGraw-Hill.

Kajüter, P. and Kulmala, H., 2005. Open-book accounting in networks: Potential achievements and reasons for failures. *Management Accounting Research*, 16(2), pp. 179–204.

Kakkuri-Knuuttila, M.-L., Lukka, K., Kuorikoski, J., 2008a. Straddling between paradigms: A naturalistic philosophical case study on interpretive research in management accounting. *Accounting, Organizations and Society*, 33(2–3), pp. 267–291.

Kakkuri-Knuuttila, M.-L., Lukka, K., Kuorikoski, J., 2008b. No premature closures of debates, please: A response to Ahrens. *Accounting, Organizations and Society*, 33(2–3), pp. 292–301.

Kaplan, R. S., 1984. The Evolution of Management Accounting. *The Accounting Review*, 59(3), pp. 390–418.

Kaplan, R. S., 1986. The role for empirical research in management accounting. *Accounting, Organizations and Society*, 11(4/5), pp. 429–452.

Kaplan, R. S., 1998. Innovation Action Research: Creating New Management Theory and Practice. *Journal of Management Accounting Research*, 10, pp. 89–118.

Kaplan R. S. and Atkinson, A. A., 1998. *Advanced management accounting*. 3rd Edition. Upper Saddle River: Prentice-Hall.

Kasanen, E., Lukka, K. and Siitonen, A., 1993. The Constructive Approach in Management Accounting Research. *Journal of Management Accounting Research*, 5(Fall), pp. 241–264.

Kaski, T., 2002. Product Structure Metrics as an Indicator of Demand-Supply Chain Efficiency: Case Study in the Cellular Network Industry. *Department of Industrial Engineering and Management*, Helsinki, Helsinki University of Technology (Dissertation).

Knecht, T., Leszinski, R. and Webe, F. A., 1993. Making profits after the sale. *The McKinsey Quarterly*, (4), 79–86.

Krishnan, V. and Gupta, S., 2001. Appropriateness and Impact of Platform-Based Product Development. *Management Science*, 47(1), pp. 52–68.

Labro, E., 2003. The Cost Effects of Component Commonality: A Literature Review through a Management Accounting Lens. *6th International Seminar on Manufacturing Accounting Research*. Twente, Netherlands.

Labro, E., 2004. The Cost Effects of Component Commonality: A Literature Review Through a Management Accounting Lens. *Manufacturing & Service Operations Management* 6(4), pp. 358–367.

Labro, E. and Tuomela, T.-S., 2003. On bringing more action into management accounting research: process consirations based on two constructive case studies. *European Accounting Review*. 12(3), pp. 409–442.

Laine et al., 2006. Accounting for networks: the consolidated network approach. *International journal of networking and virtual organizations*, 3(3), pp. 245–257.

Lewin, K., 1946. Action research and minority problems. *Journal of Social Issues*, 2(4), pp. 34–46.

Lindholm, A. and Suomala, P., 2005. Present and Future of Life Cycle Costing: Reflections from Finnish Companies. *The Finnish Journal of Business Economics,* (2), pp. 282–292.

Lindholm A, and Suomala, P., 2007. Learning by costing—Sharpening cost image through life cycle costing? *International Journal of Productivity and Performance Management*, 56(8), pp. 651–572.

Luft, J. and Shields, M. D., 2002. Zimmerman's contentious conjectures: describing the present and prescribing the future of empirical management accounting research. *The European Accounting Review*, 11(4), pp. 795–803.

Lukka, K., 2000. The Key Issues of Applying the Constructive Approach to Field Research. In: S. Roponen, ed. *Management expertise for the new millennium in commemoration of the 50th anniversary of the Turku School of Economics and Business Administration*. Turku, Turku School of Economics and Business Administration, pp. 113–128.

Lukka, K. and Granlund, M., 1996. Cost accounting in Finland: current practice and trends of development. *European Accounting Review*, 5(1), pp. 28–41.

Lukka, K. and Mouritsen, J., 2002. Homogeneity or heterogeneity of research in management accounting? *The European Accounting Review*, 11(4), pp. 805–811.

Lyly-Yrjänäinen, J., 2008. *Component Commonality in Engineering-to-Order Contexts: Contextual Factors Explaining Cost Management and Management Control Implications*. Tampere: Tampere University of Technology (Dissertation).

Malleret, V., 2005. The drivers of service profitability in small industrial firms. *7th Manufacturing Accounting Research Conference*, Tampere, Finland, 30 May–1 June 2005.

Malmi, T., and Brown, D., 2008. Management control systems as a package—Opportunities,
challenges and research directions. *Management Accounting Research*, 19(4), pp. 287–300.

Malmi, T. and Granlund, M., 2009. In Search of Management Accounting Theory. *European Accounting Review*, 18(3), pp. 597–620.

Malmi, T., Järvinen, P. and Lillrank, P., 2004, A Collaborative Approach for Managing Project Cost of Poor Quality, *European Accounting Review*, 13(2), pp. 293–317.

Mandal, P. and Shah, K., 2002. An analysis of quality costs in Australian manufacturing firms, *Total Quality Management*, 13(2), pp. 175–182.

March, J., 1987. The elusive link between information and decision making. *Accounting, Organizations and Society*, 12(2), pp. 153–168.

Markeset, T. and Kumar, U., 2004. Dimensioning of product support: issues, challenges, and opportunities. *Reliability and Maintainability—RAMS Symposium*. 26–29 January 2004.

Marshall, C. and Rossman, G. B., 1999. *Designing Qualitative Research.* Thousand Oaks: Sage.

Mathieu, V., 2001. Service strategies within the manufacturing sector: benefits, costs and partnerships. *International Journal of Service Industry Management*,12(5), pp. 451–475.

Mattessich, R., 1995. Conditional-normative accounting methodology: Incorporating value judgments and mean-end relations of an applied science. *Accounting, Organizations and Society*, 20(4), pp. 259–284.

McGovern, T., Hicks, C. and Earl, C. F., 1999. Modeling supply chain management processes in Engineering to order companies. *International Journal of Logistics: Research and Applications*, 2(2), pp. 147–159.

McIvor, R., 2001. Lean supply: the design and cost reduction dimensions. *European Journal of Purchasing & Supply Management*, 7(4), pp. 227–242.

Meridith, J. and Roth, A., 1998. Operations management in the USA. *International Journal of Operations & Production Management*, 18(7), pp. 668–674.

Molina, A., Velandia, N. and Galeano, N., 2007. Virtual enterprise brokerage: a structure-driven strategy to achieve build to order supply chains. *International journal of production research*, 45(17), pp. 3853–3880.

Morse, W. J., 1983. Measuring quality costs. *Costs and Management*, (July–August), pp. 16–20.

Mouritsen, J., Hansen, A. and Hansen, C., 2001. Inter-organizational controls and organizational competencies: episodes around target cost management/functional analysis and open book accounting. *Management Accounting Research*, 12(2), pp. 221–244.

Mouritsen, J., Hansen, A. and Hansen, C., 2009. Short and long translations: Management accounting calculations and innovation management. *Accounting, Organizations and Society*. 34(6–7), pp. 738–754.

Neely, A., Gregory, M. and Platts, K., 1995. Performance measurement system design: A literature review and research agenda. *International Journal of Operations & Production Management*, 15(4), pp. 80–116.

Normann, R., 1976. *Luova yritysjohto.* Espoo: Weilin+Göös.

Oliva, R. and Kallenberg, R., 2003. Managing the transition from products to services. *International Journal of Service Industry Management*, 14(2), pp. 160–172.

Oliver, J. and Qu, W., 1999. Cost of quality reporting: Some Australian evidence. *International Journal of Applied Quality Management*, 2(2), pp. 233–250.

Otley, D., 1994. Management control in contemporary organizations: towards a wider framework. *Management Accounting Research*, 5(3–4), pp. 289–299.

Perera, H. S. C., Nagarur, N. and Tabucanon, M., 1999. Component part standardization: A way to reduce the life cycle costs of products. *International Journal of Production Economics*, 60–61, pp. 109–116.

Raffish, N., 1991. How Much Does That Product Really Co$t? *Management Accounting*, (March), 36–39.

Reinertsen, D.G., 1997. *Managing the Design Factory: A Product Developer's Toolkit.* New York, NY: The Free Press.

Rust, K. G., 1995. Measuring the costs of quality. *Management Accounting*, 77(2), pp. 33–37.

Schein, E. H., 1999. *Process Consultation Revisited, Building the Helping Relationship*. Reading (Mass.): Addison-Wesley.

Schiffauerova, A. and Thomson, V., 2006. A review of research on cost of quality models and best practices. *International Journal of Quality & Reliability Management*, 23(6), pp. 647–659.

Seal et al., 1999. Enacting a European supply chain: a case study on the role of management accounting. *Management Accounting Research*, 1999(10), pp. 303–322.

Seppänen et al., 2002. *Kannattavuuden jäljillä—Yritysverkoston kustannuslaskenta ja sen kehittäminen*. Tampere: Metalliteollisuuden kustannus Oy.

Sievänen, M., 2004. *The Effects of Customization on Capital Goods Manufacturing Business*. Tampere: Tampere University of Technology (Dissertation).

Sievänen, M, Suomala, P., Paranko, J., 2003. Product Profitability: Causes and Effects. *Industrial Marketing Management*, 33(5), pp. 393–401.

Speklé, R., 2001. Explaining management control structure variety: a transaction cost economics perspective. *Accounting, Organizations and Society*, 26(4–5), pp. 419–441.

Suomala, P., Varila, M., Jokioinen, I., 2007. Validity problem in performance measurement: A conceptual analysis with an illustrative case on quality cost measurement. *4th Conference on Performance Measurement and Management Control*. Nice, France, 26–28 September 2007.

Thevenot, H. and Simpson, T., 2006. Commonality indices for product family design: a detailed comparison, *Journal of Engineering Design*, 17(2), pp. 99–119.

Thomas, L., 1992. Functional Implications of Component Commonality in Operational Systems. *IEEE Transactions on Systems, Man, and Cybernetics*, 22(3), pp. 548–551.

Thrane, S., 2007. The complexity of management accounting change: Bifurcation and oscillation in schizophrenic inter-organizational systems. *Management Accounting Research*, 18(2), pp. 248–272.

Thrane, S. and Hald, K., 2006. The emergence of boundaries and accounting in supply fields: The dynamics of integration and fragmentation. *Management Accounting Research*, 17(3), pp. 288–314.

Thrane, S., Nielsen, H. and Bautrup, T., 2008. Opening the books—Black boxing risk, profit and opportunism. *6th Conferences on New Directions in Management Accounting—Innovations in Research and Practice*. Brussels, Belgium 15–17 December 2008.

Thyssen, J., Israelsen, P. and Jorgensen, B., 2006. Activity-based costing as a method for assessing the economics of modularization—A case study and beyond. *International Journal of Production Economics*, 103(1), pp. 252–270.

Tuomela, T.-S., 2005. The interplay of different levers of control: A case study of introducing a new performance measurement system. *Management Accounting Research*, 16(3), pp. 293–320.

Turney, P. B. B., 1991. *Common Cents—The ABC Performance Breakthrough*. Hillboro: Cost Technology.

Ulrich, K., 1995. The role of product architecture in the manufacturing firm. *Research Policy*, 24(3), pp. 419–440.

Uusi-Rauva, E. and Paranko, J., 1998. *Kustannuslaskenta ja tuotekehityksen tarpeet*. Tampere: Tampere University of Technology.

van Aken, J., 2004. Management Research Based on the Paradigm of the Design Sciences: The Quest for Field-Tested and Grounded Technological Rules. *Journal of Management Studies*, 41(2), pp. 219–246.

Van der Meer-Kooistra, J. and Vosselman, E., 2006. Research on management control in interfirm transactional relationships: Whence and whither. *Management Accounting Research*, 17(3), pp. 227–237.

Vargo, S. L., Lusch, R. F., 2004. Evolving to a New Dominant Logic for Marketing. *Journal of Marketing*, 68(1), pp. 1–17.

Varila, M., Suomala, P. and Jokioinen, I., 2007. New Boost to Quality Costing: From Ex Post Failure Appraisal to Proactive Product and Process Improvement. *8th Manufacturing Accounting Research Conference*. Trento, Italy, 18–20 June 2007.

Velasquez, S. and Suomala, P., 2009. The search for organizational cost consciousness: An approach derived from Life cycle-Costing analysis. *9th Manufacturing Accounting Research Conference, Cost and Performance in Services and Operations*, Muenster, Germany, 21–24 June 2009.

Vollmer, H., 2009. Management accounting as a normal social science. *Accounting, Organizations and Society*. 34(1), pp. 141–150.

Westin, O. and Roberts, H., 2007, It's just a thought: acting out the "interpretative act" of action research. *8th Manufacturing Accounting Research Conference*, Trento, Italy, 18–20 June 2007.

Wise, R. and Baumgartner, P., 1999. Go Downstream: The New Profit Imperative in Manufacturing. *Harvard Business Review*, 77(Sep–Oct), pp. 133–41.

Woodward, D. G., 1997. Life cycle costing-theory, information acquisition and application. *International Journal of Project Management*, 15(6), pp. 335–344.

Wouters, M. Anderson J. Wunstra F., 2005. The adoption of total cost of ownership for sourcing decisions—a structural equations analysis. *Accounting, Organizations and Society*, 30(2), pp. 167–191.

Yin, R. K., 1994. *Case study research: design and methods*. Newbury Park (California): Sage Publications.

Zhou, L. and Gruppström, R. W., 2004. Analysis of the effect of commonality in multi-level inventory systems applying MRP technology. *International Journal of Production Economics*, 90(2), pp. 251–263.

Zimmerman, J. L., 2001. Conjectures regarding empirical managerial accounting research. *Journal of Accounting and Economics* 32(1–3), pp. 411–427.

Zwerink, R., Wouters, M., Hissel, P. and Kerssens-van Drongelen, I., 2007. Cost management and cross functional communication through product architectures. *R&D Management*, 37(1), pp. 49–64.

Index

An environmentally friendly book printed and bound in England by www.printondemand-worldwide.com

PEFC Certified

This product is
from sustainably
managed forests
and controlled
sources

www.pefc.org

PEFC/16-33-415

www.fsc.org

MIX
Paper from
responsible sources
FSC® C004959

This book is made entirely of chain-of-custody materials

#0009 - 210612 - C0 - 229/152/8 - CB